Were You There Charlie?

The Life of Charlie Card

Yes I was there — friend & neighbor

Charlie

Charles Fredrick Card

Copyright @ 2021 Charlie Card

All rights reserved. ISBN: 978-1-62269-0381

Who Will Tell Your Stories To The Next Generation?

Write Heart Memories®

Ultimate Workbooks, Published Stories & Interviews With Beth Lord
Preserving Legacy & You In A Book

206-929-0024 | www.bethlord.com | beth@bethlord.com

1/12/1937

In 1932 vaudeville actor and performer Jack Pearl became famous, launching a long running radio and even occasional movie career as his character, the Baron Munchausen, on The Ziegfeld Follies of the Air. The character was loosely based on the Baron Munchausen literary character of the time. Pearl would tell far-fetched, incredible stories with a comic German accent. When his straight man, Charlie (originally Ben Bard and later Cliff Hall) would question his truthfulness or accuracy of such a tall tale, the Baron replied with his famous punchline: "Vass you dere, Sharlie?" setting off laughter in living rooms across the nation. When Pearl would air a Baron episode, many would tune in to enjoy his tales and crumble into fits of laughter when questioned by his sidekick Charlie. "Were you there Charlie?" became the catch phrase of the day and was uttered in households across America into the late 30's and recited by many for years to come. The catch phrase continued in popularity as young children would be questioned by their parents about their truthfulness while another adult in the room would say in their best Baron impersonation 'Vass you dere, Sharlie?' and the adults would chuckle as the poor child had no idea what they meant.

Named after the famous sidekick, **Charlie Card** came to be and was born January 12th, 1937 into his own set of adventures. He may have started as the sidekick, but as you will see by the many tales of Charlie Card, the straight man becomes the Baron, living in the incredible stories he has shared with us here. Every good story deserves to be exaggerated, or does it? As you find yourself questioning, you can hear the answer back 'Were you there Charlie?' If the answer is no, you were not there – then obviously you must take the storyteller at his word...

Foreword

Granddad Edwin Card was born in Bloomer, Wisconsin. He was the only child of Jamie Card. Dad said his grandfather farmed on the Pennsylvania/New York line. There was a stone marker for the state line.

Dad said the old man pushed a wheelbarrow across Ireland to get to the boat to come to America. Granddad Jonathan Card married Ella Craig in Bloomer, Wisconsin. She was either part German or part Scotch according to what Aunt Verona said. Great Granddad's wife was a stately looking old girl and she's buried in Wisconsin, a long time before Great Granddad, born in 1842, was buried in Chelan at 85 years of age in 1917.

Granddad Jonathan and his Dad (Charlie's Great-Grandpa Edwin) homesteaded in the upper Antoine Creek near Chelan but in Okanogan County, Washington. The twins (my Dad and his brother) were born in the cookhouse at the Pennal Saw Mill, on Grandpa Card's Homestead.

Great-Grandpa Edwin was living in Chelan with my Grandfolks. They always said, *"Don't lock your bedroom door"*. The family tried to wake him one morning and of course, he had locked the bedroom door. They had to tear the door frame off to get in and the old man was dead. I found his grave marker up in the old cemetery many years later.

**Circa 1910 Ranch in Antoine Creek, Washington
Jonathan Edward Card (1941) and Ella Craig Card (1952)
Children: Ruth, Leland, Loren, Hiley, Bernice
(Before Chet and Verona were born)**

Dad had several sisters and two brothers. My dad had a twin brother. Dad was Leland Henry Card and his brother was Loren. They both went by "*Red*" because they were redheaded as all get out. I think looking back on it, most probably they both had a temper. They liked the girls and they got around a lot from what other people have told me. His youngest sister, Verona, lived to be 103.

Ruth married Roma Spray and had Wayne, Eunice, Genevieve, and Ronald. Bernice married Darwin Hughes and had Carl, Jerold, and Jan. Leland and Helen had Charlie, Bonnie, and Linda. Lorne and Edna adopted Nikki in Alaska. Hiley married Earl Bryant from Riverside, WA. and they had Roger and Paul. Verona married Dave Franklin and had Richard and Johnathan. Chester was married to Clarene and they had no children. He was the only one to serve in WWII.

Dad told many stories about his Dad and logging, cutting wood for the steamboats on the Columbia River. Dad, Lorne, and Grandpa cut the cordwood on the ranch and hauled it down with a sleigh in the wintertime to a steamboat on the Columbia River, and I guess that was quite an ordeal. According to my Aunt Ruth it was more than quite an ordeal.

Grandpa Card worked for Chelan Transfer the last few years of his life before he retired. He was sixty-four. He went hunting with one of his sons-in-law, had a heart attack and died in 1941. I've got a lot of hunting seasons since I've been retired. He did not. This was Grandpa J.E. Card. I am the last of the Cards. Well, that's the way it is, family lines run out.

Mom was born in 1910 in Lehey, Washington. That's part of Douglas County. Her father, Fred Petersen married Olive Rankin from Ferndale, Washington. Mom was Mary Helen but she only answered to Helen. Don was born in 1912. I don't know what year for Lucille and Ross.

Grandma Petersen didn't like Dad or any of the partners her kids married for some reason. Don married Evelyn Signs and had 4 children - May, Russell, Doug, and Lynn. Lucille married Vance Gideon and had Maurice. They divorced and she married Paul Urebie. They had 2 children - Audrie and Paul. Ross married Raina Overby and they had 5 children - Steve, Lester, Cynthia, Ken & John.

When Mom was five, the family went by covered wagon into southern Idaho to be Mormons. She said she walked most of the way. Well, that didn't pan out, so they came back. While they were down there, their youngest son Ross was born in Montpelier, Idaho and I think so was Grandpa Petersen. They say Grampa Pete was conceived on the boat coming over from Denmark. Mom was the only one, I think, to graduate college. And she graduated from WSC. She was a nutritionist and a Home EC Teacher but she got married too.

Grampa Pete was a steam boiler man. When the Manson irrigation was put in, he powered up to the sawmill and Grandma Pete cooked in the cook shack for the crew. Everything was on skids so they'd just skid the sawmill and skid the cook shack up to the next spot. They'd cut the timber and move on. They started back on Mitchell Creek up Lake Chelan. Later on, Grampa Peter had an apple orchard in Manson and a trucking outfit called Petersen Freight. His home was just above Rose Lake. You had to have a special permit to haul anything, and he had a good permit. So, a truck made a run to Wenatchee every day, five days a week to pick up stuff.

Announcing the arrival of Charles Fredrick on Jan. 12, 1937 weight 7 lb. 6 oz. Mr. and Mrs: Leland H. Card

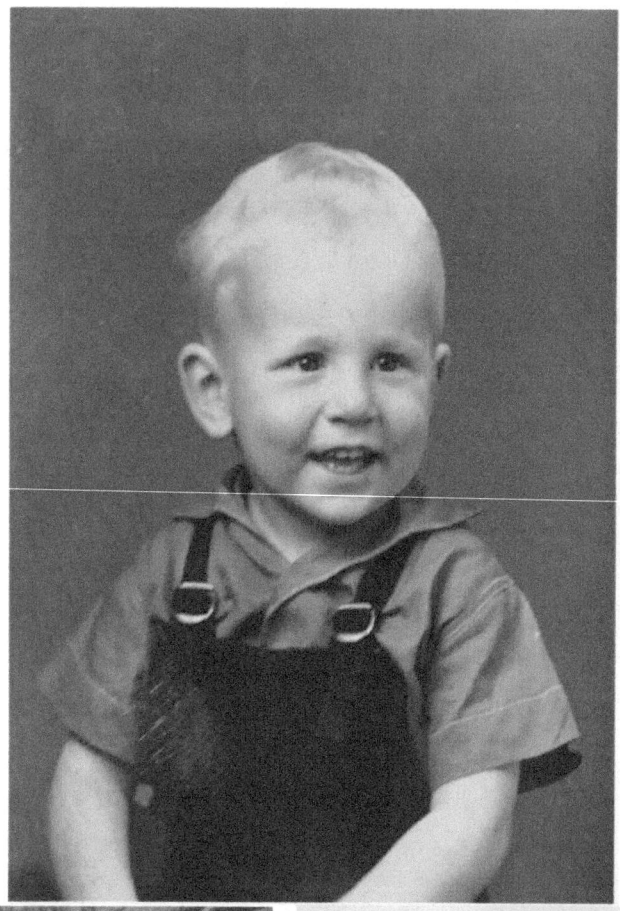

**Charlie & King
Lone Pine, WA
1938 - 39**

Were You There Charlie?

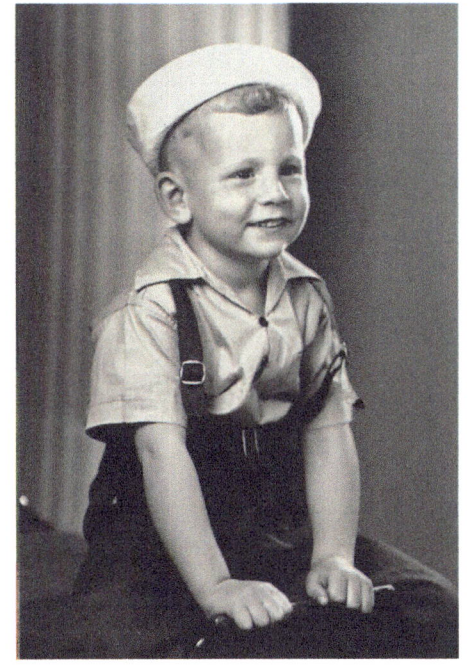

Acknowledgements

I would like to thank all the people who helped me get this book together.

Beth Lord of Write Heart Memories got me started and from there it snowballed.

Mandy Johnson was instrumental in getting me and it (the book) in order and making sense.

Aunt Verona Franklin, though long gone had some very good geneology information supplemented by Patsy Fink and sister Bonnie Cobb.

There are others who helped with names, dates and places. Especially my wife, Linda, for pushing me along and keeping things organized.

Contents

Chapter One — Page 15
First Memories

Chapter Two — Page 23
California

Chapter Three — Page 31
Riding My Thumb

Chapter Four — Page 35
Back in Chelan

Chapter Five — Page 45
The Army

Chapter Six — Page 53
Now What

Chapter Seven — Page 57
Gas Stations, College, Marriage, and Getting Settled

Chapter; Eight — Page 69
The PUD & Family

Chapter Nine — Page 85
Retired and Moving On

Chapter Ten — Page 103
My Scrapbook

Charlie's Cancer Journey — Page 141
— A note from Linda

A Prayer for Later Years — Page 147

Charlie Card

Chapter One

First Memories

I started as Charlie, Charles Fredrick Card born January 12th, 1937 in Mason City, Washington. The hospital was part of the Coulee Dam construction camp. Folks said that Charlie came from a radio show where the guy said, "Vass you dere, Sharlie?" (without the thick accent – Were you there Charlie?). And the Fredrick was my grandpa Petersen's name. that is spelled s-e-n., not s-o-n which meant he was of Danish extraction.

First Memory

My first memory was a chicken getting its head caught in the gate. My Dad (his name was Red) said something like, the SOB and then went ahead and butchered the chicken. That was at Lone Pine down the river from the dam. We lived in a little trailer with morning glories growing up the side of the trailer. We lived there my first 3-1/2 years. We moved to Chelan, a few blocks above the school in a tar paper shack. We used Grandpa Pete's truck to move there from the dam. My cousin Maurice, was there to help us unload. Two little boys weren't much help but we had fun thinking we helped. We had a woodpile, a wood stove and an outhouse.

Dad's Rules

I tried to help my dad find a place to hang his razor strap. I was told not to touch it. I did anyway. And Dad used it on me. Beth says, "Oh no" and Charlie says, "Well, I had it coming."

Charlie's Logic

One time I got a finger caught in a door in an 'ole car up there. Car doors were wood covered with a little bit of tin. I hollered for a while but made it. At four, I learned to ride a bicycle and I could pretty well get around. That first summer I caught my pant leg, in the chain on my bike. So I took my pants off and pushed my bike up the hill. By the time I got home, everybody in the neighborhood had called Mom. Well, if they called Mom to tell her about me why didn't they come out and help me?

Trow Street

We moved down to Trow Street by the time I was five, 1942, when we moved to a nice house in Chelan. I remember the lake was a big attraction for me, I could run across the lawn, open the gate and slide down the clay bank right into the water of Lake Chelan.

Chelan was a place where Indians lived and when my Dad was growing up the Indians were his friends. They didn't camp too far away when my Dad was a little boy either. We also found a lot of arrowheads and native tools in our garden.

Grampa Pete's Lesson Learned

I don't have a story about the Indians when Grampa Pete was a kid, but when he was working on Vancouver Island doing something with a whistle pump or some dawg gone thing. He was sharpening his knife and there was a Chinese Crew around him. They all got along good but Grampa pretended he was going to cut the "queue" which is the braid that goes down the center of the back of one of the Chinaman and from that day on they wouldn't have anything to do with him. This lesson taught Grampa not to mess with the Chinese.

WWII

In 1941, Dec. 7, WWII started. Folks talked about it. We covered our windows at night. The whole town was dark. The first time I saw my dad cry was when Ernie Pyle, who was a war correspondent, got killed. It shook dad up. VE Day bells were ringing and everybody was happy. It was the end of Hitler. It was time to celebrate, and the whole town went wild. I was in second grade and I had to stay after school like I did many a day. Mrs. Droppy, my teacher, went up to the principal's office to do something and came down crying. She said, "President Roosevelt has died" and sent us home.

The Lake

Every so often somebody would fall into the lake and drown. One time we were hollering back and forth across the lake to a kid who was in my classroom and he rolled into the water and danged if he didn't drown.

One time, somebody drowned just downstream from us and they had these boats dragging the water, looking like a 3-pronged fish hook trying to find that body. And they had another deal that looked like the top of an old hot water tank and it fit over a guy's shoulders a little bit. There was a glass window in it and they'd pump air into it and the guy would walk on the bottom of the lake to try and find the body. One day, these three P-38 fighter planes come up and raised over the bridge and dropped right back down by the water and then up and over the dam and they were gone. I found out later they crashed in Moses Coulee Creek when they plowed into a wall because they couldn't get up quick enough.

In 1945, a school bus went into the lake. It was a narrow road and it had been snowing. People figured, later on, a rock came down and hit the front tire. The bus driver wasn't going very fast but he probably tried to stop and when he did that the bus skidded into the water in one of the deepest parts of Lake Chelan. I had three of my second cousins on the bus and only one came up. It sent the whole town into shock. They had barges and navy divers looking in that water. They got the bus up but they didn't find all the kids. Thirteen kids died on the bus as well as the bus driver. About that time my appendix was acting up and Doc Bridgem hauled me down to Wenatchee and took it out at the hospital. The first night at the hospital I walked up and down the hall and found a nurse sleeping and I bopped her on the head. The nurse and I had quite a tussle but she got me back into bed and Doc Bridgem came in the next morning and he told me in no uncertain terms that if I got out of bed again, he was going to tie me into the bed. Dr. Bridgem brought me back from Wenatchee to Chelan, the day they had the funeral for the kids that had drowned on the bus.

Babysitters

Dad hired a housekeeper while Mom was in the hospital after Linda was born. Bonnie was two and I was seven. I didn't like the babysitter so I ate a raw egg in front of her. This smoked her up real bad and so she quit. I don't know who took over from there but maybe mom was home from the hospital in Wenatchee. Norm Evans, the boat race driver did a lot of babysitting for us when we were little. I kept track of him most of his life since he raced hydroplanes all over the place.

Boats

Most people had rowboats. Dad had an inboard (a speed boat) and we had a dock. Old Man Bolyard had a boat, an old tub, that didn't run and it was tied to the edge of our dock. I was an ornery little kid so I dismantled the engine by putting a pipe on a wrench like I had seen my Dad do. Bolyard came by and told my Dad I had dismantled the engine but my Dad didn't believe him. But I had done it. I had taken the head off the engine. I never told Dad that I had done this. Eventually, Mr. Bolyard and the tub went away and freed up our side of the dock. We lived between the bridge and the dam. Now the house is between two bridges and it's built-up so much I couldn't find it even if I tried.

Shenanigans

Patterson's had an old livery barn just up the road from our house. It had a hayloft in it and a rope tied to the top of the barn and that was a wonderful place to play. Get up there. Get up on the rope and swing back and forth and see how far you could jump in the hay on the other side. It was just the attraction for little boys. On the ground level, there were horses and harnesses, and an old, old car. The tailrace of Chelan Dam was another neat place to play. The guys I played with were in high school and I was in grade school. Linda calls in the background, "Charlie was a little hellion." I don't go back to Chelan. It's a long, hard three hours. When my Dad's youngest sister was alive I would go back there to see her but she died three years ago at 103 years.

Charlie, Grandma Pete, Bonnie, Mother, Dad, Grandpa Pete, Linda in front of house on Trow Street, 1947 - Chelan

Charlie, Bonnie & Linda.

Trow Street, Chelan 1947

Chapter Two

California

We Left Chelan when I was in 4th grade in 1948. Dad bought a truck down in California and drove it back to Chelan. He built a bed and sides on it. We put all the furniture in it and I slept in the back of the truck at night. Mom drove the Model A Ford and Dad drove the truck. I picked up lots of flintstone and arrowheads while waiting for the *Mary Hill Ferry*. I walked on the beach and found more than a sack full of arrowheads and flint chips. This was very exciting for me. We were in Oregon and I found a big 'ole piece of pumice about the size of a 10-pound bag of flour and it was so light it would float. I put that up in the back of the truck. We were somewhere in the central valley of California and I was talking to an old man and I took the pumice and threw it at him and said, "*Here, catch it*." He just about had a heart attack getting away from it. Dad had a pretty good talking to me then. I brought the pumice back into the truck and I had that thing for many years because I had a rock that could float. Most people in southern California never saw a rock that could float.

San Marcos

We made it to San Marcos. Grandma and Grandpa Pete had a little place between San Marcos and Escondido.

They lived there in the wintertime and went to the ranch in Canada in the summertime. That's what drew the folks down there. I went to school in San Marcos. The school had an outhouse and a red clay roof.

Home

Dad had bought a little place of 10 acres with two milk cows and an old Cletrac tractor. It had a nice, redwood barn for hay and a milking parlor. I learned right away how to milk and squirt milk in my sister's face and the cat's mouth. I was ambidextrous so I could get them with either my right or left hand. We had a creek running through our place, running along the edge there and it was full of crawdads, turtles, and bullfrogs. The bullfrogs could stretch out 12-13 inches long and that's a measurement I remember. We would go out at night with a flashlight and jig them with a three-headed spear. We'd skin 'em and Mom would cook the legs. That was great fun.

School

It was a mile to school so we would kick a can back and forth so it wasn't a bad walk. I was always trying to learn something. In the fifth grade, I learned a lot about magnetism and electricity. The teacher had just gotten out of WWII and he was an interesting teacher. Our sixth-grade teacher was an old, worn-out Opera singer, Miss Seagull. She was an interesting person - always getting carried away with her high opera voice and singing. In the seventh grade, we got our eyes open by our teacher, Bob Burzil. He had been a star football player for San Diego State. He had also been a P51 fighter pilot and a prisoner of War. It seemed like he knew everyone. And he exposed us kids to everything you could imagine. He knew a lot about The Orient because he had been there. We made a big mural at the end of our classroom. Once we had a big luau. We roasted a pig in the ground. He took us to the San Diego Zoo. Even the people at the zoo knew him.

We went to places nobody got to go - inside the snake house and in the back where they took care of the penguins. Our parents had to sign release forms because Bob was going to get us rides in an airplane maybe. There was no maybe. He had it cooked up. One of these days we left San Marcos. It was only 35 miles to San Diego. He took us to Lindberg Field which is the main airport in San Diego. We got off the bus and there was a DC3 sitting there all cranked up and ready to go. They loaded us on it and we flew northeast over Palm Springs and every kid got to sit in the co-pilot seat. That was a big deal. We were seventh-grade kids and we had taken in a lot.

Then Bob introduced us to the Starlight Opera. We got to see *Annie Oakley*, *Mikado* and *Oklahoma* on stage. The *Mikado* was a Chinese play. It was funnier than ever and they were using different lights to change the looks of the performers. You put one light on a performer and their dress was red. You put another light on the dress and it was green. That was interesting for us.

Making Money

All this time I was milking cows at home and for the neighbor. I got paid for milking the cows at the neighbors. I got seven dollars per head per month. He usually had two or three head. That gave me a little pocket money and when I walked across the pasture some mornings especially after it had rained, I could pick up these little white mushrooms and I'd pick them and Old man Crider would give me 50 cents or a dime, for them. I thought that was another good deal.

Bicycle Adventures

We went to this little lake, called it Thibbie's pond. It stored water for a walnut grove. It was on our neighbor's place. Jimmy and I'd bale hay for him in the summertime and we'd go over to his pond skinny dipping and cleaning the dust off of us and have a good clean up. There's a hill, coming down from the pond and a 6" or 8" pipeline ran along the edge of the hill. We'd ramp up so we could ride over it and jump. When we were going up the hill, of course, we had to pick up our bikes to go over the pipe. One day I was jumping over the pipe flying high and the front wheel comes off. It was a sudden stop that yanked my bike up in the air and twisted it up pretty bad. I looked a mess but healed up. Just before Christmas in 1952, I was going down a slight slope on my sister's bike. I had worked on the gears a little bit so it would fly downhill. I hit a rock probably the size of your fist. It crumpled the bicycle up real good. It skinned me up pretty bad on that old gravel road and I broke my right hand.

Another time I rode my bicycle across the San Marcos tracks and I broke the crank right in the middle. It set me right down in the middle of the bike. I didn't think I would ever be able to father a child. ... I guess I never did. It sure hurt and I laid along the side of the tracks moaning for a while and then pushed what was left home.

Watermelons

In San Marcos, there was one store that had a post office and everything. in it. Then there was a little bitty feed store and the feed store was also a hardware store to boot. The guy that owned the grocery store had watermelon and we kids went in to buy a watermelon. He charged us seven cents a pound for that dang thing. We very carefully cut it into five or six pieces, ate the pieces and put it back together again and wanted our money back. He gave us hell and we got out of there.

That's when pop bottles were worth a penny to return and we would find pop bottles and return them too.

Catching Skunk

It wasn't too long when I was helping a guy in his lemon grove. I don't know what I was doing but there was a skunk there. I smacked him with a lemon. I knocked it out. I took that skunk and rode my bicycle back at night after dark and pitched that thing on the roof of the little building in San Marcos that had the store and the post office. The skunk hit a wall and landed on the awning over the front door. Nobody would be able to see it on the second floor unless they opened the window. It stunk so bad nobody got their mail for a few weeks. As I said, *"I was an ornery little fart."*

Movie Stars

I was extremely busy. I knew everybody. If I wanted to go to a picture show I'd ride my bicycle across the tracks, around this little hill and then I'd thumb a ride into Vista to go to the movies. And then I'd try to get a ride back. One time I got a ride with a guy and I was telling him all about the movie I was going to see. He let me out there and I went to the show and that guy was in that movie. I don't remember who it was but I was all excited about that. *Fred Astaire* lived on my Dad's feed route and *Leo Carillo* was down the road from us just a little way. I saw *Fred Astaire's* three legged-dog and the guys who took care of his place but I never saw *Fred Astaire*. There were a lot of the old Hollywood stars that lived around us.

First Shotgun

I went to Rich-Mar grade school and graduated in the eighth grade. Then I went to Escondido Union High School. Our bus driver was Art Hallis and he was the greatest guy I knew. The bus was so crowded it would have taken three buses in today's world with the laws we got now. The last batch of kids on the route had to stand up. He'd go clockwise one week and counterclockwise another week so we alternated between a short ride and a long ride to school. He owned a sporting goods store and that's where I bought my first shotgun.

Driving At 14

I got my driver's license when I was fourteen. It was restricted to driving only farm stuff so I always had an axle or a crankshaft or something that needed fixing in the car with me. I didn't abuse this privilege.

Escondido Union High School

They had a merit/demerit system where the school gave you a hundred merits to start the year, and if an upperclassman caught you in the hall doing something wrong, you'd get a demerit. In my sophomore year, this kid broke the lead in his pencil so I loaned him mine. He scribbled down the homework assignment; the bell rang and he went off with my pencil. Previously, I had gotten 20 demerits and if I got anymore Dad would have to sign me in. Dad had already told me if I got anymore demerits he wouldn't sign me back into school and there'd be hell to pay. In the next class, I didn't have a pencil., and the old girl gave me five demerits. So I bid her up to about 50 more demerits. I got up to the wood shop which was my next class. I was pretty pissy by then. Smitty was a good teacher but I locked him in the paint locker and he gave me more demerits. I didn't have any more merits left. It was February, 1953 and the next Monday was Lincoln's birthday and we had the day off. I took off and never went back to that school ever again.

Chapter Three

Riding My Thumb

Getting Away From Home

Johnnie Green had a '36 Chevy. I threw my clothes and shotgun in it and we took off for Texas because his mother lived in Dayton, Texas and he wanted to go down there so away we went.

Abandoning The Chevy

We broke down at Bakersfield, Texas because we threw a rod out of the old car and it bounced on the ground until it couldn't drive anymore. We left everything in the car we couldn't pack and hitchhiked into Bakersfield. Bakersfield was just a T in the road with a post office and that was it. We tried to hitchhike out of there and finally, six or seven sheep trucks went by and the last one picked us up. There was an old guy in the truck who had tobacco juice running out of both sides of his mouth and down over his shirt. He had a month's worth of beard on his face and wasn't the best kept guy, kind of wild looking. He was telling us stories about his drilling wells and water for his sheep with that damn oil coming up. Johnny and I just sat there laughing because this guy is full of BS. We got to Sheffield and there's this great big white Cadillac and this 'ole girl crawls out of that Cadillac with a little fur coat on and comes over and plants a kiss on daddy. We found out his stories were no BS at all. Everything that 'ole boy told us was the truth.

Texas Country

We bought two tickets to Dayton from Sheffield on the bus and that took all our money. I wired home I was going to another school. Texas was kind of a funny country because you had to buy a glass of water for a nickel because it was so dry there. Can you believe there were kids there that had never seen it rain?

Working There

Johnny's Stepfather worked in the Baxtor sawmill and they ran on Saturdays. They were usually shorthanded so he got me into working there when I wasn't going to school. I was either tailing the edger or pulling on a green chain. They cut big timbers for oil well construction. I also got another job working for a rice farmer and I worked three days for him plus the weekend. I'd take turns weekly going to school and working. I bought a 1929 Chevrolet car with the money I had made and as soon as school was out, I sold that car for twenty-five or thirty dollars.

Traveling Around

I hitchhiked to St. Louis, Missouri and went up the Mississippi River Valley. Of course, that was an adventure in its own right, but I also got stopped in

Louisiana and that was an adventure that could have turned ugly. I got stopped there by the police. There was a bank hold up and two cops thought I could have done it but one of the cops realized I was just a big old dumb kid going along and he let me go. The next bunch of cops come by and hauled my butt off to the Parish jail because they don't have counties and they fingerprinted me. The first cop came in and told the others to let me go because I wasn't the guy. That was a relief when they let me go. I hitchhiked up to St. Louis because I had a friend at Scott Air Force Base in Illinois. I hung around there for a few days and then I decided I'd hitchhiked to Denver, Colorado because my Dad had a sister there.

By The Grace Of God

I stopped in Columbia, Missouri and bought a great big chunk of watermelon for a quarter. Watermelons were floating in big old water trough of ice and man, that was good. I caught a ride out of Columbia with a man who had a brand new little 1953 Chevrolet car. This guy was taking it back to a rental outfit or something. We were going along and I had my arm out the window but the Lord told me to pull my arm in just a second or so before this car swung out so fast to pass us that it turned into us and took the right side of the car off. But my arm was where it belonged and not laying on the road.

Denver

Dad's older sister and her husband lived there and I had two cousins there too. I stayed there for a few days. Jerry, the second, oldest boy was going to get married in Portland. He had rented a house and he had to clean it up so I told him I'd help him paint it and get it ready for his bride. I rode with him to Portland, Oregon. After the wedding, I hitchhiked to Sultan and stopped because friends of my folks lived there. He had had a little dairy in Grand Coulee where I was born. I stopped in there and he had two semi loads of hay there to unload. So I worked inside of the barn and they would put the hay on the elevator, and I would take it off and stack it. That afternoon we got it done, I went in and laid down on the register in the house and went right to sleep I was so tired. Mrs. Marshall woke me so I showered, cleaned up, ate a bite and went back to sleep. The next morning I got up and headed for Chelan.

Chapter Four

Back In Chelan

I hitchhiked back to Chelan. In those days you could go anywhere with a thumb. I got to Chelan and saw my cousins, and they had a friend there - Dud who had just quit Bob Kercheval's Ranch and he said they were looking for a hand so I hitchhiked out there. It was ten miles out of town and I went to work there for room and board and $180 a month - changing sprinklers and putting up hay. I was sixteen and it was between my sophomore and junior years of high school. It was 1953. I was strong as a bull and dumb as an ox. I was the guy who fed the elevator and two guys stacked 1200 bales of hay in one day.

Grandpa Pete Died

Along that timeframe on July 8, 1953, my Grandpa Pete died in British Columbia on the X Bar J. My folks came up to Chelan for the funeral. I had pretty well decided to eat crow and go back to California and live with them. Well about five minutes, just talking to my dad I figured no way in hell would I ever live under his roof again. My Dad wasn't mean but it was his way or the highway and I chose the highway.

Going Back To High School

I continued to work on the ranch I was on at Kercheval's - putting up hay, changing sprinklers from five in the morning until you fell over at night. When the school bus came by that fall, I just went out and got on it with the Tester and Zornes kids and went into school cold turkey. I'd gone to school in Chelan until the fourth grade, so I picked up where I left off and knew a lot of the kids. I had two cousins going there.

Deer Hunting

In high school, I went deer, bird and duck hunting. I only got one buck but lots of ducks, quail, chuckers, pheasant, and grouse. In the spring we hunted groundhogs and around here they call them rock chucks. They're lowland marmots.

The Packrat

When I left Kercheval's I lived with the Testers who were neighbors in the Antoine valley for a week. And then I moved up to Tom Meyers place which was an old cabin up on the hill. The sun only shined a few days in early December and January. It was a cold place but it had a wood stove. There was an outhouse, wood stove, and no electricity. I got by fine. There was also a packrat in there. I heard him scurrying around at night and one day that son of a gun stole one of my socks. I didn't have very many socks so I took a bead on that sucker and shot it. I got my socks back and a whole bunch of other stuff that'd been missing that I hadn't missed. I never missed anyone as much as I did that damn pack rat because he was the only living thing around there. He was scurrying around all the time at night. And then it was silent. That was one of my mistakes. I killed that packrat and I was lonely.

Mike Paul

I was running around with Mike Paul who was probably the smartest genius I've ever met in my life but he had zero common sense. None. He was always building some dang explosive, mixing chemicals because his Dad owned a drug store so we'd build bombs. These were dry elements we would transfer from paper to paper being gentle and careful or the paper would sparkle and such. One time, Mike concocted this thing and I took a 2-inch pipe and put a cap on it, a plug on one end with a soda straw and a firecracker on the other end and made a pipe bomb out of it. You had a minute to get away once you lit it.

We took it up back of Azwell. That's a little town between Chelan and Pateros. We went up this little canyon I knew about because it was near Kercheval's Ranch. It was night. We set this pipe bomb on a big rock there, put some mud around it and torched that sucker off. The bomb went off and it made a pretty big bang out of it. It cracked the rock. The next morning, the first person in the gas station was from Azwell and asked if I felt the earthquake that happened around 1:00 in the morning. This person said it was so big that it shook him and his wife up. I called Mike after he left and told him what this man said so Mike pretended he was a geological surveyor from the University of Washington and called people to see if anyone else had felt this big bang around 1:00 in the morning. Mostly, people said no and we had a good laugh over it.

We both had Model A Ford Coups. We sure kept the town busy but never doing anything too destructive. One time, Mike torched an explosive up in a vacant lot across from his house and it broke windows for four blocks. The police and neighborhood had a gathering at the station and Mike's mother was trying to put my name on this situation but I had an airtight alibi because I was at Larry Getty's house studying and Larry's mother was home.

Mike graduated from Annapolis, top of his class but he got his diploma withheld for three months for misconduct. He wound up a frogman out of Coronado, California. *He was awful hard to handle.* He did so many tricks and was a skirt-chasing son-of-a-gun. In the last fifteen years of his life, he drove a Taxicab in Mill Valley, California and loved it. We kept in touch. He died of brain cancer. I don't think he put his smarts to very good use.

Hitchhiking Back To California For Christmas

Still, I'm 16 and I'm helping Tom Meyer when I decided I would hitchhike to California for Christmas. I caught a ride with Bill Glass and he took me clear down to Bakersfield. I hitchhiked down to Escondido. The folks had sold the little farm and moved to town. I didn't like milking cows anyway. I stayed there over Christmas. I had bought a bus ticket to go back to Chelan. which cost me 35 dollars. Dale Yetter was a friend of Dad's from Chelan and he was visiting Dad. He bought a car in California and wanted to keep his other car too so he asked me if I would drive the car back to Chelan. I felt rich. I had 35 dollars in my pocket because I returned my bus ticket and I paid for the gas and my food. I drove that car back to Chelan in the winter, before I turned 17.

The Bluebird Café

I moved into a little cabin behind the Bluebird Cafe that Lloyd Morton owned. I helped at the bluebird cafe, kept the wood stove in the grocery store chock full of wood and whatever else I could do to help pay my rent.

Herman and Ezola Schultz lived across the alley right by my cabin and I got acquainted with their three kids - George was a year older than me, Barbara was two years younger and Evie. I've been friends ever since. The day Ezola died was the day I felt my mom died because she was kinda a mom to me. Every time I'd get out of line she'd be on me like a dirty shirt.

Mike Harris's Cabin

I don't know but for some reason, I moved down to Mike Harris's cabin. It was three doors down the street from the cafe and not far from my uncle Earl and cousins, Roger and Paul Bryant. It was a neat place and a really interesting experience. It didn't have a shower or heat but it did have an oil cook stove that kind of kept the place warm. I lived there until the end of school. It had a toilet that looked like a big funnel and the seat was set up at an angle. You sit on the seat and water started pouring on you and swirling around your butt and washed it. I lived there until school was out.

X-Bar-J For The Summer

When school was out I hitchhiked back to Canada and helped my uncle working there. Gram was always cooking at the X-bar J. My uncle Pete and Aunt Raina were down at Westwold in a log cabin on a gravel road a mile off the main road and by the river and had three little bitty kids. Pete and I hayed there for another rancher. I entertained them by the river and cut wood. There were lots of mosquitos, oh boy. When fall came, I rode my doggone thumb back to Chelan.

What I Need To Graduate

I went in to see the principal and he said "Charlie, according to all of my records, you have never taken any physical education." I needed PE credits to graduate. He said play football in the fall for your senior year and that will take care of your PE credits. Playing football my senior year cut me out of a lot of work. It cost me a lot of money because I couldn't work and play football at the same time. It was Apple Harvest of course and I couldn't work as much so it dipped into my money. I practiced football four days a week for two hours each day and then a game on another day. We were the Mythical State Champions of 1954.

Mrs. Riddle

The principal said I couldn't live alone anymore. He didn't think it was good for me. I think he set it up for me to live with Mrs. Riddle but I was never quite sure. I went out to see her and she wanted 40 dollars a month for room and board and she didn't do laundry. That was the best bargain of my life and I hopped right on it. I gave her the 40 dollars so fast it wasn't funny. Her boys didn't do anything. Two big kids one older than me and one younger than me but both bigger than me. I took care of her lawn, shoveled the snow and all that stuff. She did my wash because I always helped her.

Between the kitchen and the living room, there were grates with heat coming up from the furnace that was in the basement. That's where I sat and did my homework. She always had lots of cookies in a gallon mustard jar and I sat there eating and doing my homework. When I ate all the cookies up, the only thing she said was "Do I want some more cookies?" Mom and Grandma were never like her. They'd get angry if I ate more than two cookies at a time.

Art Garton

I was working at Art Garton's gas station which was also

a machine and mechanic shop. I called over to Glass Grill and ordered a hamburger. Bill's wife called and said my hamburger was ready so I ran over and got the thing. I got back to the shop and Art was there. I bit into my hamburger and there was no meat in it. Art grabbed that hamburger and charged right across the street and we had a good laugh over it. That's where I got acquainted with Bill Glass. Art was one of my favorite people all my life. He was a lifelong Democrat but if he were alive now I don't think he'd be a democrat because he wasn't liberal. I still visit his son regularly.

Odd Jobs

I went through my senior year there, working in the cemetery and working at Art Garton's gas station and working at Foster's Butcher Shop. I picked up jobs everywhere. In January of 1955, Leonard Little, an accountant who traded at the gas station brought me my w-2 forms. There must have been 19 of them. He says, "I'll do your taxes if you take care of my car," and that's what we did. I worked cleaning, gardening and any other job I could find.

I'm 84 years old and I have never done my taxes. I always get an accountant to do it. Leonard taught me that, you do what you do and I'll do what I do and, that works.

Charlie's Senior High School Picture

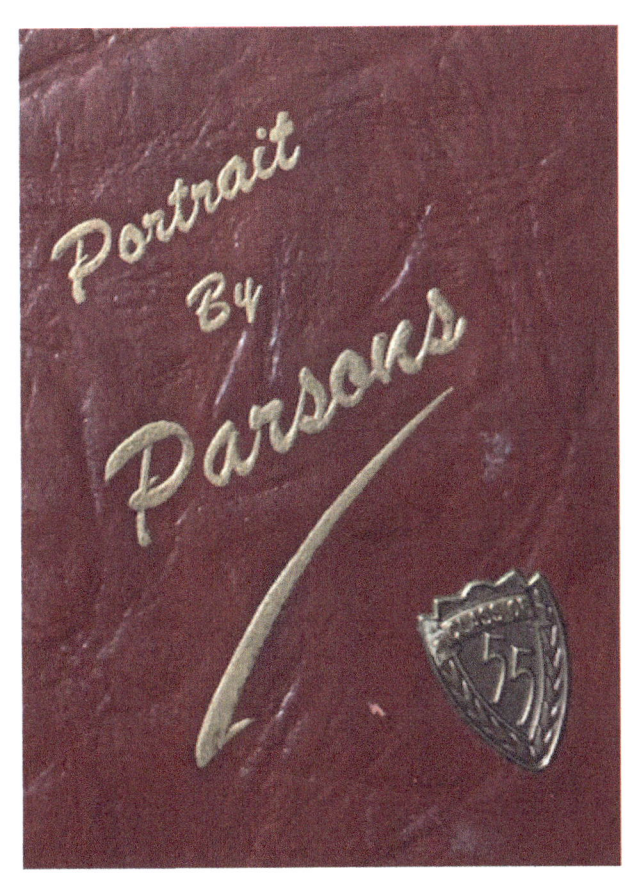

Charlie Doing his Job As A Gas Station Attendant

Chapter Five

The Army

I made it through the school year and I got my draft notice the day before I graduated out of high school. I had thirty some days before I had to report to the draft board in Wenatchee.

I rode my thumb to the X-Bar-J again and worked for twenty-seven days up there and then hitchhiked right back down to Chelan. Artie took me down to the bus station on July 6th. It was a long slow ride to Seattle. I went through processing and the army said, "*Yep, you're fit.*" and I was in the army. Off I went to Fort Ord in California. It's south of San Francisco.

Private Card (1955)

We flew in a DC3 from Fort Ord to Burbank and landed for some reason and then landed in Kansas. They got us off the plane, walked us around, fed us two sandwiches and got us back on the plane to Fort Knox, Kentucky. And that's where I took my basic training. I was in D company of the 23rd armored engineer battalion, 3rd armor division.

Tractor Scraper School

The army saw I was a farm boy (*most of us were*) and I got sent to Fort Leonardwood, Missouri to a tractor scraper school. I was pretty used to tractors anyway, it was a natural for me. When I got out of that school, I had about four days to get back to Fort Knox, Kentucky.

Spare Time

I just decided, well, heck with this, I'm going up to Peoria, Illinois to the caterpillar tractor plant. So I hitchhiked up there. One farmer picked me up and I said, "You know, I don't want to be left out in the boondocks. Give me a good place to catch a ride." He said he'd do that but he left me out on the corner of a cornfield, corner of a cornfield, corner of a cornfield and another cornfield and we're talking mid-November in the middle of the night. I gathered corn stalks and stacked them up along the side of the road and built a fire. A couple of cars go by and pretty soon a rig comes by and picked me up. I was colder than heck by then. I got into Peoria and spent two days wandering around The Caterpillar plant then I hitched back to Fort Knox.

Fort Knox

When I came back I had a D7 Cat assigned to me the whole time I was in the service and it was pretty good duty. At Fort Knox, we built bridges, built roads and fixed what the tanks tore up. Then they shipped us to Hanau, Germany in late May or early June 1956 and I got on the troop ship, USS Hodges, with about 5000 other guys.

USS Hodges

They asked for volunteers for the kitchen duty while they made up the duty roster, I volunteered. I took the garbage and dumped it off the fantail of the ship and that's the way you did it by throwing everything overboard in those days. So as I did that I saw there was a guy standing there, splicing cable and I watched him and said, "Hey, you missed a tuck there." He turned to me and he said, "You're the kid I'm looking for, we've got to re-rig these lifeboats and I need somebody to help me." So he got a hold of my company commander, and I moved out of the troop compartment before I ever got settled in there and wound up in the crew's quarters. I had my own room. It was a good deal. I spliced cable and worked on ropes the whole trip over in ten days or whatever it was and I didn't have to go down to that dang stinking troop compartment.

Hanau, Germany

We were in Hanau, Germany, not too far from Frankfurt. That's where our barracks were and they had been built by the Germans. They were first class masonry with granite steps all the way to the third floor. The steps were indented a little because the Germans wore hobnailed boots.

I had a lot of fun at night. Linda wants pictures of me when I was in the army and I couldn't find any without girls in them. Linda says with a smile, "It was terrible." The only decent picture we could find was a little kid sitting on my lap." Linda said, "It's better than a girl" and Charlie said, "It's a matter of opinion."

We were fixing things all over Germany that the tanks had screwed up. The tanks can really mess things up. They bumped a barn and knocked it off its foundation. So we put it back, just exactly as it was so that meant wooden pins and no nails or bolts and things like that. I was in Germany for a year.

Charlie holding a kid at Klein Karbon

They sent Stan and me out to a little bitty town called Klein Carbon. He was my running partner whose responsibilities were a truck and a trailer. Mine was a cat. The town wanted us to build a sports plotz. And the army told us when we left that the town was pretty heavily leaning toward the communist way and not to offend anybody. We put French drains in this field. The Germans hauled the gravel there, and then we covered it back up with dirt. We lived with families there and that was fun.

Stan could play anything with strings on it, so it wasn't long until Stan was playing his guitar, mandolin, fiddle or some dang thing. I went along with him and we made lots of friends and had lots of fun. Both of us got hooked up with girls, of course. It lasted that long and that was the end of it. We got the Sports Plotz built, and on the fifth of May, they threw a party for us guys who had come out here and built that sports plotz. I drank a lot of hard cider while I was there and the towns people called it Apple Voy. They crowned me Mr. Apple Voy and gave me a medal. A few days later, we shipped out.

And low and behold when we shipped out of Germany we were on the USS Hodges again, on that same ship. I walked up the gangplank, one of the ole seamen saw me, yanked me out of the ranks, and brought me to the first mate and I never did have to go down in the puke hole. It was a sweetheart deal. I really liked the water. I guess I should have been in the Navy.

I never had to be with the troop below. I had my own room, a shower, and the whole nine yards. There was a box of apples in the companionway by the kitchen that came from Chelan Apple, packer # 56 had packed them. I wrote the number down for some reason. When I got back to Chelan I ran into Dewey Haiter who was one of the bosses out at Chelan Apple. So I asked him who was packer 56 and he said, "That's my wife. Why?" I told him that we had eaten the apples she packed, and it was a little bit of home in the middle of the Atlantic Ocean 5,000 miles away. And his response was, "Oh My Gosh." Charlie says, "You just don't know how you touch peoples' lives.

Chapter Six
Now What?

X-Bar-J

I mustered out of the army at Fort Lewis, Washington, in June 1957. I hitchhiked down to Art Garton's where he was working in Olympia for the state doing something. I stayed with them for a few days because they were going to go back to Chelan and I went with them. I got back to Chelan then headed straight, by way of my thumb, to the X-Bar-J in Canada. It was northwest of Kamloops on Dead Man's Creek. The old house had been built in 1886. Gramps and Gramma had a guest ranch, and we packed fishermen in and out on two different lakes. We had a rowboat there. People could stay in the cabins, fish and grandma even cooked for some of the bunches.

Horses

I planned to work at the ranch and eventually buy it. Maurice, my cousin, and I would build things like a haystacker. We'd put up hay, packing fishermen into the lakes, making sure the 25 head of horses were taken care of. We'd use them for packing and riding. I came out of the lake one moonlit night, seven horses behind me and riding ole Nellie when a white short-horned steer jumped out in front of Nellie. It spooked her. I was sound asleep so I got up off the ground and I had horses strung all over the place that I had to untangle because they had been tied together from head to tail.

I took some horses to the lakes and packed in some things and there was a boy who was there to unpack the seaplane when it came in. I was chewing on some Copenhagen and I gave him some and told him to tuck it under his lip and chew. When he felt there was enough juice to spit, then spit. I padded him on the shoulder and by accident, he swallowed the tobacco and in a short bit of time, he was a very sick little boy. So the seaplane came in and I had to unload the supplies and haul them back to the cabin.

Crookedness

These Union Reps came up from San Francisco and they would tell me how they made extra money. They'd borrow money from the retirement fund and build a bowling alley. I asked them why they built a bowling alley. And they said they could change it into a strip mall in nothing flat or a warehouse or anything you wanted. Then they'd put the money back in the coffer. The whole idea was the union bosses would make sure there were no labor problems.

This was a crooked union. There was no doubt about it. The contractor would get a contract and need so much equipment and the union reps would buy the equipment and rent it to the contractors. When the equipment was paid the union reps would sell the equipment, and pay back the pension fund. They would take what was left over and build bowling alleys.

Change

One day my Uncle Pete showed up at the X-Bar-J. He was working on pipes at a pumping plant for the Trans Canada oil line at the time. He came up and said, " I sold the place to Fergusons so you guys (my cousin and me) better pack up and get out of here." So Maurice and I packed up and there I was without a job.

My uncle's family came down to Chelan and ended up in Caldwell, Idaho and my Gramma had a little apartment in Manson above the post office and would wander around visiting my folks in California and Pete's family in Idaho. Maurice went to California where his mother lived.

Charlie Card

Chapter Seven

Gas Stations, College, Marriage and Getting Settled

Chelan

I hitchhiked back to Chelan and went to work for a gas station again for Happy Harry. I was making 45 dollars a week and I thought I was in fat city.

Gas stations were real service stations. People would come and I'd go out and pump their gas, get under the hood and check their oil, fan belt and water. I'd wash their windshield and vacuum the car which was real service. We would also sell people items they might need. Come along fall, I went to college. When school was out I went back to Chelan and got a job building a bowling alley.

College

So I went with a cousin of mine and started at Central Washington College of Education in Ellensburg, Washington. I lasted a few semesters. I didn't have any money even though I was working every chance I could get after the first year so I decided to go back to Chelan.

Work And Marriage

In Chelan, they were building a bowling alley and I showed up. I asked if they needed any help and they said they did so they paid me a buck an hour. During that summer I got married to Cassie. I had known her in high school. She was raised on a homestead that my granddad had homesteaded in The Antoine.

Bicycle Accident

The last decent bicycle I had I used to go to work building the bowling alley. I was living in an apartment not too far from where the bowling alley was being built. The bowling alley wanted a broom finish so I grabbed a broom. I was riding my bicycle holding the broom over my head to get to the construction site. Two walnuts were hanging from a tree asking for a dumb kid to take a swing at them so I hauled back and took a swing at them. There was a damn limb hooked on to those walnuts and it tipped me over. I looked like I had been sorting wild cats. I got skinned up and it was a doozy.

Cassie And I

Cassie and I met through a mutual friend, we hooked up and got married in Sept. of 1958. We had a 1936 Ford pickup truck. Cassie and I lived in an orchard cabin then. I went back to Central for another fall quarter and Cassie stayed in Chelan and packed apples. I was fighting for grades and trying to make a living and it wasn't working so I dropped out of college and went back to Chelan. That Christmas we drove to California so my folks could meet Cassie.

Working

I worked in the sawmill, a gas station, and as a printer's apprentice for a while. It was hard to get by on a buck an hour. The printer was paying a buck an hour and the sawmill was paying two dollars and a nickel. I went to Babe who was the owner of the printing place and I asked him if he could raise it to a dollar and a half because I couldn't make it on a dollar and he said, "No. It's a dollar for six months, that's what it's going to be." So I put together the paper for the week and then went to the sawmill. I was the littlest kid working in the box factory but the money was good. We made box shook (slats) for Del Monte. I didn't like the guy I was working with so I quit. I drove an apple truck for harvest.

Rumblings Of A Ranch

I was working in the gas station again when Cassie and I leased a ranch which had about 250 acres. My buddy Mike showed up from Annapolis and he's got a couple of weeks just to screw around. The first thing he wanted to do was shoot a deer so he poached one and I said I'd see him out there next morning and he said he didn't want to do that again because it wasn't fun. So we had to cut the deer up, wrap it up and put it in the freezer. Deer meat was our staple.

We went to Anaheim lake which is up in Central British Columbia. I had an international truck so the three of us piled into the truck and we went to Anaheim Lake. It's about a hundred miles of dirt road from Williams Lake. We took a kayak with us. We got bored fishing because you could catch fish all the time. We'd go down to Dean River where it flowed out of Anaheim Lake and you'd catch a fish on a fly and keep using that fly until you were sick of catching fish.

One time we took a Canadian boy with us to scout and we're paddling down The Dean River and we see a bear on the shore. In those days, a bear was definitely considered a predator. Mike said he'd shoot that sucker, so we steadied the kayak. He fired and shot the left eye out of the doggone bear. I was eating a peanut butter sandwich and Mike was trying to get a decent shot at the bear. The bear is swimming in the water right there in front of us.

He smells me and he gets his front feet on the front of the kayak right over the top of my legs and scratched the kayak all up. I dropped my peanut butter sandwich into the water, stuffed the kayak paddle in the bear's mouth and pushed him over backwards. Mike was still trying to reload the gun, and he had bullets in the air, bullets in the boat, bullets in the water, but none in the gun.

The Canadian kid couldn't swim a stroke but boy did he want out of that boat. I'm the only one with the cool head. Mike shot the bear where I told him. We skinned it out and brought half of the bear meat home - all the good stuff. We brought the heart and smoked it when we got back to camp. Smoked heart tasted good but we gave the rest of the meat to the Canadian kid who was running the camp. He was mystified by the event the crazy Americans pulled. He was up for the summer taking care of the camp for some people in Vancouver and we paid him a dollar a day to camp. It was a pretty interesting trip all the way around. I didn't have time to smoke the rest of the bear because I had pulled the water off the hay to dry and I had to get back to cut the hay.

The ranch had 54 decent acres for alfalfa. The rest of it was steep rocks with 15 - 20 acres of flat top and was hard to get at. It was dry land so I went up there and planted a bunch of wheat. In those days, the farming association would come out and measure it. If I planted too much; I had to disc some of it up. As I went up the hill to get a tractor from the neighbor who had a tractor with a big disc on it to do that, I saw cows in the wheat field. The cows must have broken the fence down. They were Les Swanager's cattle and they had taken care of the wheat so there was no problem anymore but here were a couple hundred cows eating my grain.

So I went up to see Les. The insurance man had come to see me. I remember he was a big, tall guy, skinny as a fishing pole. He chewed some sort of plugged tobacco. He said, "The average county wheat that year is 20 Bushel to an acre and the price of wheat is 4 dollars to the bushel so how 'bout I write you a check for that 15 acres of wheat that the cows ate?" So I got the money for the wheat and I didn't have to harvest it. I didn't have to do anything with it. That all worked out pretty well. I come out on the sweet end of that deal. I sold my first crop of hay at $20 a ton. That was a penny a pound. I didn't do a very good job on the hay. I lost a lot of leaves.

Our First Home

We were out there a couple of years and I wound up working in town at another gas station and I bought a house in Chelan for $4,000. You got to remember this is 1959. I bought that house and it wasn't too far from the gas station so I'd walk back and forth to the gas station to work. Well, cement and my old legs couldn't take it. And my brother-in-law says, "Hey, come on down to St Helen's, Oregon and work in the sawmill for a while." So I went down there where he was at, and worked in the sawmill and Cassie stayed in Chelan and packed apples.

I was home one weekend and I ran into J.L Johnston. He was a good contractor. They were building the approaches to BB bridge at Chelan station. He said he'd remember to hire me. A few days later he called the gas station and they called me at the sawmill. J.L told me they'd hire me so I quit the sawmill right in the middle of the shift. The guy at the sawmill said, "You can't do that," and I said, "I seen you can guys in the middle of the shift so I'm doing what you normally do. I was a hard son of a gun. I went back to Chelan in my old 1937 Chevrolet 2-Door sedan and my German shepherd dog, Shep. Oh man, would he stink because he only ate venison or grass. Shep would stick his head out the window and howl.

The Wenatchee Fire Department

I went to work for JL Johnson Construction as an oiler (a grease monkey) and worked on the tractors, the cats, and stuff like that. He laid off in the winter because of the snow but I'd blade the big road and open it for the other contractors because they were still working and building the forms to the bridge so I'd go down there once a week. It was a very rough environment. I was drawing unemployment but he paid me a little bit under the table so I could grade the road. Then there was an opportunity to work for The Wenatchee Fire Department. There was a bunch of men they tested and they hired four of us. I was one of the ones they hired.

So I rented a house near the fire station in Wenatchee because you had to live real close to the station and I rented my house in Chelan for forty bucks a month. I was paid two hundred a month from the fire department. The first six months you paid on your house were considered a down payment so as soon as the Chelan home's six months were up I bought another house in Wenatchee. I paid six grand on Pear Lane for it. It was a little more than half an acre so it gave me room for a garden. It was in the county but surrounded by the city. I lived there for two years and when Patty (my daughter) was just about two, I bought another place in East Wenatchee.

Fishing & Hunting

While I was on the Wenatchee Fire Department I did some Steelhead fishing and some bird hunting. In the early 1970's I started elk hunting. On one trip, we left early one morning in a Jeep Wagoneer. We were four men and a teenager. And I shot an elk down in the canyon and the guy with me did a lot of shooting but he never hit anything. He hiked back to the jeep to get somebody to help. He's a heck of a nice guy, but he was not in very good shape so he sent a younger man to help me pack out the elk. The young guy got down there and it was snowing, blowing and dark. I was down out-of-the wind sitting there roasting a piece of elk meat.

He got there and he roasted some elk meat and we were quite comfortable. We took off and hiked back towards

the jeep with part of the elk. We got back to where the jeep was and there was no jeep. The other guys had moved it about a 1/2 mile down the road. That young guy was madder than hops. We got to the jeep and the road was most full of snow, but the guy driving the jeep thought we'd be fine but he got us stuck by being timid so I had to dig it out. I dug us out and told him exactly what to do. Then he got us stuck again within 15 or 20 feet. I dug it out again and when I got done telling him what to do, he really understood.

We got out of the road tracks on a flat land where there was scrub sagebrush, rocks and stuff. I'm using a penlight to spot rocks and stuff like that, and I missed one and they hung the rear end up on it, twisted the drive line. So there we are, no driveline and no tools in basically a blizzard. I been up a long time so I dozed off a little bit and the next thing I know, the other men got the dang jeep running and the heater was on and they were huddling to keep warm. I got out and had a little pruning saw with me and cut some sagebrush, piled it up and got a fire going. This time, I'm getting tired so I fall into the jeep and the next thing I knew the fire's out and they're all in the jeep. So I got out, cut some more brush and built another big fire. Got them all out and got them around the fire. I went back into the jeep and got a little sleep again. I was pooped from doing all the

walking I had done. Next thing I knew, I woke up and the fire was out, they were in the jeep and the jeep was running so I give 'em hell.

It was starting to get daylight so I said, "let's get out and walk boys. We got no business setting here." We walked two to three miles and finally ran into some guys in an old jeep and the side story on that is I went to school with one of those guys in that jeep. We drove to the Game Department and called our wives and they came and got us. A couple days later, the weather let up and we went down to where our jeep was. We got the meat and packed out what was left of it. Took the driveline off the jeep and drove it home on the front axle, the front wheel drive, and made it home fine. Lance, the teenager had carbon monoxide poisoning and puked and puked and puked. Then the other guys were all pretty well washed out. I think carbon monoxide poisoning played a big part in that. I saw that the muffler had a hole in it. That's the last time I went hunting with that trio.

After that, I started hunting with three men from our church. I used 2x2's and made a tent about 20 feet long and sixteen feet wide, put eight-foot walls up and covered it with clear plastic. Fixed a place for our stove in it and we had our camp set up. We hunted like that until I retired. I used my saddle horse most of the time to hunt because my legs were never that good. One of the guys wanted a horse and told me to bring one down. So I lined up a horse, had it shod which was forty dollars or something. I had to take extra hay and grains for the horse. We finished hunting and the man offered me a twenty. And I just said, "keep it." I just never took another horse in for him when we went hunting. He had no idea what I'd laid out. I know for a fact he was in better shape financially than I was.

Charlie, About 1985

Change Again

The Fire Department was working out pretty good and then on St. Patrick's Day the Chief walked in. He said we have to lay three of you guys off. I was one of the last three hired so I was done.

I was a little bit pissy about it. I went down to the unemployment office. The guy at the office said there were no jobs but I still had to fill all the papers out and he said he'll see if he can get me a job. I said "I can get a job before filling them papers out." He laughed and said, "Oh no you can't." So I went back to the house, made one phone call and went to work the next morning for a bricklayer. I was packing bricks, mixing mud and what have you. I was working long hours.

Charlie & Cassie, 1958

Chapter Eight

The PUD & Family

Getting The Temporary Job That Lasted Until I Retired

A kid called me up named Larry and he was one of my high school buddies' brother-in-law and he said, "Do you want to go to work for the PUD? They got a temporary 60-day job out here at Rock Island Dam." So I went down and saw the hiring boss and he said, "Sure, I'll be glad to have you." So I went out to the dam to work on the gate seals. There were prints to work from but the journeymen couldn't figure out how to build the wooden blocks that would hold the seals on the bottom of the gates. I had taken enough mechanical drawing classes in high school so I started figuring out these blocks, how to do it and drawing them. The next thing I knew we were done with the Gate Seal job and they put me on a gardening crew for awhile. If you go to the Rocky Reach Dam and look down over the side of the dam just by the fish ladder, you'll see three interlocking circles down there. Well, I built them on the gardening crew and they were only supposed to be temporary. It's held up all these years

Becoming A Lineman

Another job came up from PUD in Wenatchee. I bid on it and got it. It was a permanent job. I was a ground man on the line crew. I liked it but one day they sent me over to the auto shop to help out. I had spent enough time servicing rigs and things like that so I fell right into the swing of things. One of their mechanics had gotten hurt so they just made a mechanic out of me. They liked me and even gave me a raise but I knew I'd be stuck there forever and there wasn't much opportunity. I wanted to get back to the dam because I thought it was a better place to be. So I went back to the dam and I was a utility man cleaning things, checking the fish ladder and I stood that for three years.

Becoming A Father

We adopted a little girl, Patty. She was born in 1966 when we were at the Calgary Stampede. We got home from the stampede and a woman from the Children's Home Society called and said our daughter was here. We had to go to Yakima to get her. She will be 53 years old at the end of June (2019). We were really prepared; Charlie laughs. We dumped everything out of one of the chest of drawers and fixed a bed in it. A doctor friend who lived up the road had 4 girls and his wife brought down clothes to last the kid for about 8 years old so we lucked out there. Work called me up about 5:00 and said, "They had something for me to do at the fish counter shack." I rode my bike out there and they surprised me with a baby shower. That was a neat experience.

Life changed drastically because I had always had a job that I could quit. It scared the thunder out of me that I had a job I couldn't quit. I was obligated for 18 years. I'd put Patty in my old pickup in a basket and we would drive back and forth from Wenatchee to the Antoine (her gramma's and grampa's place- my wife's folks place). I'd go up there and bale hay, do whatever needed to be done. We'd head back and Patty would always wake up once we went through the tunnel. I'd haul her back like that 25-30 times that year.

We got Mike two years after Patty (1968). He was a month or so old when we got him. There was something in his heritage somebody didn't like, maybe his Indian blood, who knows. We didn't care. We wanted him as a son.

Buying Another House

I bought another place in East Wenatchee and I paid an astounding $12,000 for that. It had three acres on it, a good view and just a nice little shack. It had a few apricot trees. I planted some apple and cherry trees and a big garden. Right after I bought that, I was still working at Rock Island Dam as a utility man. I was working shifts where you were ten on and four off - ten swings, ten graveyards in ten days. So you never knew whether to go to the bathroom or go to bed. It was a horrible deal.

Any time I had a few minutes I'd drive the 55 miles to my brother-in-law's ranch and help him out. I finally got burned out on that after a couple of years. I went back to being a part of the PUD line crew and I was a grunt there for about six months to a year. I got my apprenticeship and came out a journeyman lineman several years later.

<u>Being A Good Neighbor</u>

The neighbors had Homer Moser build a house for them. Two or three of the Wenatchee firemen I used to work with were helping him. So Homer hired me in my spare time and when I went back on the line crew I took two weeks off in the fall to help Homer frame a house. That way he had something to do for the rest of the winter. It was hard work. In my spare time I helped him build more of his house. The house had a lot of angles in it so it took a lot of time. Homer was a true, blue, honest to God, Christian. He lived it, acted it, showed it in everything he did. The next thing I knew my wife and I were baptized.

Red, Charlie, Helen, Cassie & Patty, 1967

Raising Kids

When I was raising our kids, I had a little Livingston boat and we could launch the boat a couple miles away right there by my house in East Wenatchee and we'd fish The Columbia River. The most fun we had is that I'd stand in the back of the Livingston with the tiller of the outboard motor in my pants leg so I could steer it and my son would stand in front of the boat with the electric touring motor. And we'd go around the edge of the river shooting carp with a bow and arrow, and that was a hoot. We even got one rock chuck. But shooting rock chucks in rocks was not a very good idea because it messes the arrow up.

Patty was interested in horses and later on in boys, but mainly horses. I was Mike's Boy Scout Leader. Mike was a car nut. We also hunted quite a bit. We used to be able to hunt deer with either a rifle or a bow. There'd be a bow season as well as a rifle season. We'd go hunting during bow season and then we'd go during the rifle season. The law changed and you couldn't do that anymore. We were hunting on Birch Mountain which is just north of Wenatchee. Mike had gotten a deer with a bow. We were on horseback and there was a yearling on my right side. So, I stood up, twisted myself around in the saddle to get the young deer and I did. It dropped right then because I had hit the main arteries on both legs and it bled out in seconds. I thought it was pretty good that I had actually killed a deer off a saddle horse.

Junior Rodeo

We got pretty active in the church. The church wanted me to help build the church. I told them at the church I wouldn't work on the new building until I was done with junior rodeo. My girl loved horses so she got involved with Junior Rodeo and so I did too. I helped with junior rodeo's and finally I put on a junior rodeo in Cashmere. I also helped in Eastern Washington Junior Rodeo Association. I was its first president. I found out last year it's still going strong.

Church Building

The first weekend I was done with the rodeo I went out working on the church building's foundation. It was a Chinese fire drill. Guys would dig a ditch and somebody would come in, cover it up and pack it down without getting the pipe in. Nothing was getting done. I went to the elders and said there had to be a better way so they said I could figure it out. I got a friend, Curt, who was a paraplegic. He broke his neck body surfing. It didn't hurt his mind or his arms. We figured out a schedule to have a good crew.

If you helped on the crew the first and the third Monday in the month that was it. If you worked on the second and fourth Monday of the month that was it. We figured this out and lined up a bunch of crews. I'd go out in the morning with the contractor we had hired. He'd say he'd do this in the morning but in the evening he hadn't done a dang thing. So, we did what he was supposed to have done plus what we were supposed to have done. I put up with that for about a month and then I went to the elders. I was smoked up and said, "Can him." And they said, "We can't do that, he's a nice guy." I said, "I don't care if he's a nice guy, can him because I'm tired of doing his work too." One of the members of the church was a contractor but he couldn't work for 2-3 weeks until he was finished with the building, he was on so we mucked along until Mike Fowler (the new contractor) came. We worked good together.

Our crews worked well because you didn't get worked to death because you only had two evenings a month to work and people liked that. By the time we got the church building put together, I didn't want to see another church building in my life. It pretty well burned me out. It's just a building, the church is the people.

I found out my talent is scrounging. I knew a lot of the Seventh-day Adventist boys and they'd leave their equipment right there by our building on Friday night and wouldn't be back to get it until Saturday night or Sunday morning. They had their backhoes, and stuff like that so I would ask to borrow it on the weekend. There was another guy who was a contractor and his father-in-law belonged to our church and I got pretty well-acquainted with them. He had a big crane and several big pieces of equipment. He would just bring them out there and leave them for me.

The only restrictions he put on me was that I was the only one to run the crane setting the beams in the church building. So I had a D6Cat out there, 710 John Deere hoe, and a big pavement compactor all in one weekend. I knew these people and I had balls enough to ask them if we could borrow the equipment. I don't know how much money I saved our church building but it was a lot. My daughter was the first one to get married in the church.

Both my kids grew up to be independent. Patty works for Burlington, Northern Santa Fe and lives in Great Falls, Montana. Mike is a stay at home dad taking care of an autistic son. He's a journeyman electrician and lives in East Wenatchee.

Mike – 7th Grade – 13-1/2 y.o.   Patty – 10th Grade – 15-1/2 y.o.

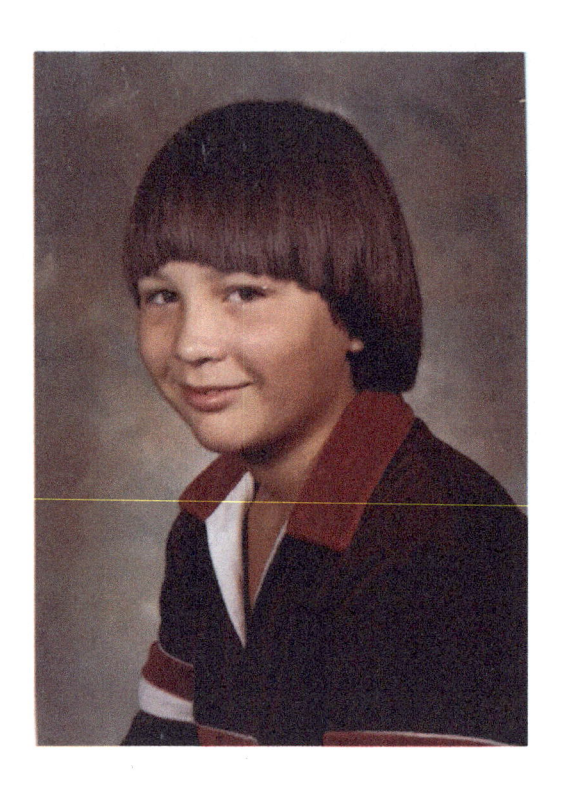

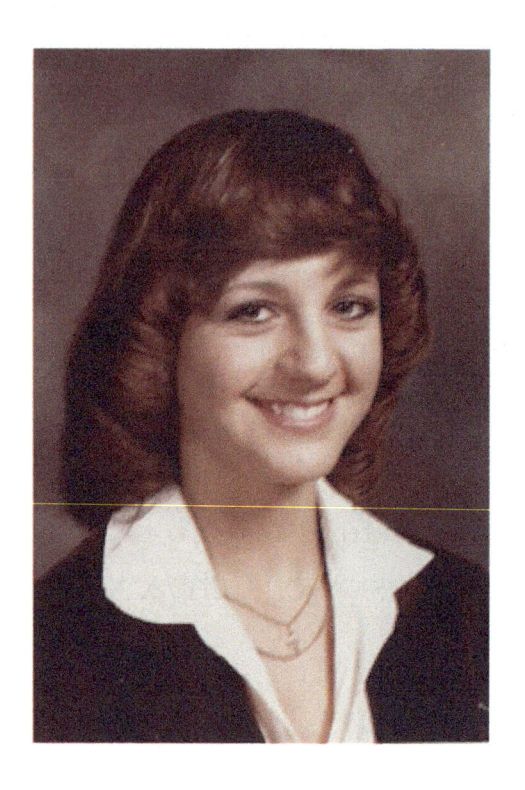

Patty and Charlie 2016

Mike and His kids

Front: Helen (Mom), Red (Dad)

Back: Bonnie, Charlie, Linda

PUD

I worked with PUD and I was a line foreman. Then I got a serviceman's job which was a lot better because I didn't have a crew I had to worry about, keep track of and keep out of trouble.

When I was a serviceman, the Entiat River froze over and it froze from the bottom up. It was really cold. The county came to me about blasting ice out of the river because it was starting to flood the roads. I got a hold of a friend who had taught a couple of blasting seminars. He came over and we lined out about a quarter of a mile of that river. We got the local volunteer firemen to drill holes in the frozen river and we got a bunch of 2" peeler cores from a veneer mill at Omak. We stuck 2-3 sticks of dynamite in the holes, and primer cord coming up and we got it all ready, tied it together and shot her up. It raised up and down at the lower end the river was open and flowing into the Columbia River so the ice started flushing out. The next day all the ice was gone so that worked out pretty good.

I retired in 1992 at the age of 55 from Chelan County PUD. I had a lot of fun working for the PUD. I did a lot of the rock blasting. Blowing up rock was a natural for me and I had done it in high school with Mike, in the army and now for PUD. I was also a line foreman and then a serviceman taking care of the small things.

I guess I could have worked another ten years but the kid I had trained who was a nice kid became boss and turned into a jerk.

Charlie, circa 1990

Decorating a Christmas Tree

Benton REA 1992

Chapter Nine

Retired and Moving On

Retired

I retired. I bought a new Dodge pickup with Cub Cab - a decent pick up with a camper on it. So Cassie and I went off on a big trip clear across to Maine and up into Canada. We traveled and did lots of trap shooting and sightseeing. There was always new road, new country and we met lots of people in 1992. Cassie and I drove to Halifax, Nova Scotia across Highway 2 and the Northern Tier Highway in the United States. Then we came down through Washington DC and spent a couple of days there. It was time to vote. I had picked out a place in Missouri to have my mail sent to and get my ballot so I could vote. Then down to Arizona and home. By the time we got home I was done traveling. We had seen a lot of country.

We still had the rental house in Wenatchee and Chelan. Cassie convinced me to sell them and I wish I hadn't because their value would have increased and I could have hired someone to manage the properties. Oh well, we make mistakes and learn.

Change

Somehow I wasn't in love with my wife anymore. I was

just indifferent. And the more indifferent I was, the worse it got. Of course, the kids were raised and on their own. I went back to work.

Working In Construction

After I retired from PUD and we got back from our big trip, I went to Oaxaca, Mexico in September, 1992. I went there to put in a water system in a little Indian village up in the hills, away from just about everything. They flew us up in an airplane and we landed on a dirt strip. It was just a flat, dirt field and we hiked down the hill three or four miles and set-up camp in an old, adobe, school house there. We put in a water system from a spring up on the hill down and around the houses. We couldn't put a spigot by all the houses because we didn't want people jealous of who had the water spigots so we put the spigots in the middle of the houses so no one got upset. That was quite an experience with three other guys from our church. Oaxaca was an interesting town with the people, the farmers and the marketplace. People bought food every day at the market and didn't store anything.

The next year my son and I went to Romania to help an orphanage. By this time, he was a journeyman electrician and I was a handyman. They didn't have power lines we could work on so we spent most of our time fixing toys for the kids like swing sets, slides and stuff like that. We had to pay our way there, pay for room, board, food and work for free. Who does that? We did. It was quite an experience. The people made it worthwhile. We were getting ready to leave and one little boy who tagged along with me didn't want me leaving. It broke my heart.

I came back and one of my brother-in-law's, Tom, asked me about the Romanian Orphanage. He just cut me off and tried to tell me all the stuff he'd seen on television. But that news didn't match my experience there. The news was wrong. My brother-in-law didn't want to listen to the truth.

I went back to work as a lineman in Steven's county. We called it, The Republic of Siberia that winter because it was cold and snowy. I enjoyed different challenges like this one.

I then went to work for an old friend of mine from Wenatchee. I ran a robotic wheelebraider and it threw steel pellets at the wall of water tanks, took the lead paint off the big storage tanks and stored it in bags and we disposed of it accordingly.

Nothing To Do In Prosser

I wound up down in Prosser as a lineman. I didn't have a dang thing to do at night. One of the other guys from Chelan County was there and in my camp, but all he wanted to do was sit around and drink beer. I needed to do something. I met Linda, the meter reader from the

Benton REA. She was there to show me the lines I had to work on. In my spare time, I helped Linda with her place which was a little out of town. Before I knew it, I was involved with Linda.

Going Back To Wenatchee

A friend of mine who lived in Wenatchee had work for me to do so I thought I'd try that and get away from the temptations of Linda, *the Meter Reader*. That didn't help. I also worked in a couple of trips in Alaska and one to North Dakota to work too. By that time I was pretty well hooked up with Linda and so that's when things fell apart with my marriage. It had been in the process for a long time. I divorced Cassie and I will take the blame for it. I didn't do right by Cassie. Cassie stayed in East Wenatchee. She stayed there with her siblings to watch out for her mom who lived nearby in Chelan. Now Mike is watching out for Cassie. I saw her last year at one of the grandson's high school graduations. If somebody dies up there she'll call and tell me. She'll send me obituaries of people and information about people because we knew a lot of people in the church.

Setting Up Home In Prosser

I came back to Prosser and lived with Linda while I worked for Franklin County PUD, Wilson Construction and the REA doing different line jobs. I was 62 working for Wilson when we completed a substation at Umatilla

Ammunition Depot and that job just about drove me crazy. The government was always in your business at that job, looking under your car for oil leaks. That didn't set good with me and they bitched about me throwing stuff in their garbage container and then they decided we weren't union. I went down there one day and I got the union steward and the big boss and another guy at this construction site and everybody had their name tag with a picture on it and the date of birth. I looked at them and said, "You know, I've been paying union dues longer than any of you sob's have been alive so don't start hounding me." We got that ironed out and they left me alone from then on out. I married Linda in 1996.

Cattlemen's Association

Moving to Prosser and living with Linda I became a cattleman as she was very involved with the Benton County Cattlemen Association and the Washington Cattlemen's Association. We went to all the local meetings and state conventions.

I went through the local chairs becoming Benton County President. Later I was District 5 Representative. All this time Linda was Secretary.

In the late nineties the WCA had trail rides. They were several days log and put together by a group of Cattlemen from the northern part of the state. They were always a lot of fun and we made some of our best friendships there.

Remaining active in WCA & help with Farm

Farm Fair is where 5th grade kids are bussed to the event and given a small introduction to many facets of agriculture. Each group has a booth and 8 minutes to tell their story. Then the kids move to the next booth. Of course mine was cattle. I feel this was the best time I spent for agriculture. The feedback from teachers and kids was fantastic.

This ultimately led to the Agriculture Hall of Fame. I was inducted into that in 2011. Linda put together a scrapbook of my journey through life and agriculture with letters of recommendation from past and present WCA presidents, friends and neighbors. *See documents in Chapter 10 Scrapbook.*

It was a very humbling experience to be included with the likes of State Senator Veloria Loveland and Bud Mercer. Through the Cattlemen there were many trips to Olympia to speak to the legislators on livestock and agriculture issues and for Beef in the Capital Day. They would line up for a block to get a small barbecued tri-tip, beef slider, asparagus, chips, cookie and milk. The favorite day in Olympia.

Salmon Fishing

I stopped hunting when I retired. I did go hunting one more time after that with my son, his wife and Linda in Montana. It was freezing and it was a very cold experience. I lost the will to hunt, and I haven't fired a gun in several years.

Les Petersen, my cousin said, "Come up to BC and we'll go salmon fishing." So we went up to Vancouver Island and stayed at a fishing lodge. We took his boat a couple of times but then we found out we could pay a guide to furnish the boat, the food, the bait and everything and just bring our clothes. This was fun and probably just as cheap. We still go fishing there. I've made a lot of friends. I just go over on a two-hour ferry ride to Nanaimo. Invariably somebody shows up that I know. People say I must know about 20 percent of the people on Earth. Well, I don't know about that, but having never met a stranger, I probably do know a lot of people. I've never hurt for friends. I could walk into downtown Seattle and probably make a friend in five minutes. It's just my nature.

Hot Air Balloons

There was the yearly Prosser Hot Air Balloon Rally, and I helped a guy put his balloon away for the night. The next day I asked for a ride and went. This turned out to be Vic. He and his family have become good friends because of this yearly event. We went flying out here one day from our property and we flew over a piece of ground, five acres that I'd been trying to buy for years and the guy kept screwing me around. Vic is married to Mandy who is a good businesswoman and gets things done. The man had put the land with a real estate agent and he wanted $5000 earnest money. Vic went down and gave it to the attorney and said, "Let's get going on this." Mandy got that place bought for less money than we offered for it. It's adjoining our five acres right behind it just to the west. And all they do is fly out of it once or twice a year. They come over and set their camper up. We run the cows on it and before they come we get the cows off and clean it up so Vic and Mandy thinks it's wonderful when they come. We put an irrigation system on it. They built a little shack just to store stuff in.

We've flown so many times we can't count the times. They flew a balloon over the top of Mt. Rainier and we were part of the chase scene when it got to the ground back in Gleed just short of Yakima. That was an experience worthwhile.

One time we took off in front of Cesar's house. We went due west for about two miles. We were fifteen hundred to two thousand feet and raised to five thousand feet. We caught an east bound wind and came clear over our place and over Prosser, let down by the football stadium at Prosser about fifteen hundred feet again and landed within 70 or 80 feet of where we'd taken off. They call that boxing the field and very few people have ever got the privilege to do that here. One other flight, we got out real early in the morning and set up in the dark (known as a Dawn Patrol flight) and flew down by where the balloon rally was going on. We lit up the balloon by putting propane in it and the heat made the balloon rise and light up in the dark. We gave everybody a good show. Then we went over and touched down in the river (known as a splash and dash) just touching it slightly and picking up and setting over where we started out.

Charlie and Vic Johnson ready for lift off 2012

We got a lot of people involved with ballooning in one way or another. We used to have a big balloon party here, but that fizzled because it got so the locals would furnish all the food and do all the work. The balloonists were just dropping in; some weren't even invited and sometimes someone had shown up who had been drinking and that didn't cut it. I'm not a tea totaler but one beer is absolutely enough, a small glass of wine or maybe enjoy a small glass of whiskey. There's that gene in the Petersen family for alcoholism and I don't want anything to do with it. I wouldn't take a chance on it.

Charlie and Vic ready for lift off 2020

After flying you can get together and laugh and tell stories.

I like to tell stories.

A Good Fit

I raised lots of hay and did ranch stuff all my life so Linda's ranch grew on me. This was a good fit. After all my jobs I stayed home and started helping Linda around the ranch. It made sense for me to ranch and raise cattle.

We have put together a nice little ranch. We added to her old home, built a hay shed, put a new steel roof on the house and barn. We added about 20 acres, all grass for our cattle. I got involved in the Washington Cattlemen's Association. We have the beef butchered right here.

Cesar

I'd hire kids off and on. One day I told the Ag teacher I needed a kid to help me and Cesar Godinez showed up. He was 17 and just a nice, quiet Mexican boy (born in Yakima). We built a straw bale building and he just kept doing chores, and any other thing that needed attention. I told him to find a job where he could work more and he said, "I'm fine here." The kid grew on us. One day his dad said, "We had saved his life because he thought he was going down the wrong track."

Cesar earned several scholarships and went to Universal Technical Institute in Arizona to become a mechanic. Cesar had a buddy, Miguel, going to UTI and they roomed together. Cesar came home at Christmas to our surprise. Miguel drove up in his car, and totaled his car less than fifty miles from home. After Christmas, Miguel rode back to Phoenix with Cesar. Later, Miguel's Dad found a car and took it to Las Vegas. Cesar, Miguel and another boy drove up from Phoenix to Vegas to get the car. Cesar and the other kid had to get back to work in Phoenix. Miguel was supposed to sleep, and come along the next day. But being a kid, he decided to drive back alone. That was his last mistake.

Cesar took care of all the arrangements in Arizona. Miguel's Mom, Dad and his two sisters met Cesar in Arizona to take Miguel's body to Zacatecas, Mexico. One of his sisters, Maria, was a teenager. Two teenagers together for that long trip. A year later Cesar and Maria were married.

After graduation Cesar couldn't get with the company he wanted because of a speeding ticket he had gotten while in high school. He went to VW Tech School and then he had to work a year in a VW shop in Alexandria, Virginia. We went there to see them. Maria was 8 months pregnant, but still she showed us all over D.C. When Cesar finished his obligation at VW; Cesar, Maria, and Little C went to Winchester, Virginia because that's where Cesar's folks had moved.

We arrived home in good shape. Two days later while I was at a WSU Experiment Station for a meeting, I passed out. I spent a long night in the hospital. After which I called Cesar to come home but he had already promised his Dad's boss he would work for him for two years. A promise is a promise with that kid.

Two years later, he and his family showed up in Prosser. We had our rental ready for them. Cesar went right to work for RDO - a John Deere Dealer in Sunnyside. Maria went to work at the farm where her parents had worked and had grown up. After a few years renting, I said, "You've paid enough rent for your down payment on the place." We sold it to him for about what I originally paid for it.

While in high school Cesar had bought a heifer and a steer calf. The steer helped him pay for UTI. The cow has done really good for him. He and his kids own about 1/2 the cattle on the place now.

We became grandparents with Cesar's kids. This is very rewarding. Little C and I are together all the time. A daughter was born to Cesar and Maria 4 years later. Carla is a little pistol. I see Cesar and his children every day because they live only two hundred yards from us. The kids have calves too so you can see that the boy has green ear tags in his calves and the little girl has red ear tags in hers.

Charlie Cards current most important project.
Grandpa to Cesar Miguel Godinez (Little C). Little C is a shadow and has gone from a good little helper to an integral (not so little) helper.

Little C (4 yrs. old) & Charlie, 2009

Little C (11 yrs. old) & Charlie 2016

Little C (16 yrs. old) & Charlie 2021

After a day of work Cesar came home to a surprise—his Dad visiting from Virginia!

Cesar Godinez, Cesar M. Godinez, and Andres Godinez
Prosser, WA March 2020

Petersen Family Reunion, 2018

Last summer we had a family reunion with the Petersen's at Sedro Wooley. Boy, it was a hoot and we had a real good turnout. After the party was over, Linda, Les and I piled in my pickup and we went back to the X Bar J in British Columbia. We had a flat tire, thirty-five miles off the pavement but we managed to get the tire changed and get out of that predicament. We got to the old ranch house, but it was showing the signs of wear. In the late 1800's, they just sat logs on big rocks. The woodshed and outhouses were all gone. The old pump house was leaning very badly. One of the cabins was still usable and it looked like some guys had been using it for a hunting cabin. The icehouse was repairable in a week's time with two people and lots of money. The tack shack's floor was pretty well gone. You could see where saddle racks were and that was about it. The old barn was twisted and broken. The blacksmith shop was gone, and the corral you'd put the horses in was fallen down. It would have been a disappointment to my granddad or my uncle if they had seen it. When we left it, it had looked like a golf course. It just went to pot.

Storytelling

You don't ever want to get me started telling stories because one story reminds me of another and another. When I was up fishing in BC, I'd get to telling stories and somebody would say. "How do you remember that?" See, someone would be telling a story and that would kick one loose in my head. I can't remember what day it is but I can remember some useless yarn.

I'm 85 years old. I've always had a good job, reasonably good health and I raised two kids without them ever getting into too much trouble. I've been married to two pretty decent women. The one I've got now pushes me an awful lot and I get tired but that's just the way it is. I go to aqua-aerobics three days a week. Two old men besides me and a bunch of older women and some are

even older than me. Some of them are heavy. I've stayed the same weight all my life - from high school to now but I'm not as tall as I used to be.

Come out here and I'll show you what a good piece of meat tastes like because we raise our own meat. It's grass-fed and never had anything to make it grow faster.

I have lived the best life ever - missed the depression, WW2, Korea, Vietnam and always had a good job and nice family. What more could a man ask for? You know, it's been a wonderful doggone life. It's been charmed and I am content. It's been a good life.

Do you have hate in your heart? Because some people start off hating people, hating groups of people and I don't understand this. I get to know people one on one, not groups. I gotta make some Amish Friendship Bread. You make two loaves and give one loaf to a friend with the sourdough starter and recipe and then they pass it on.

Keep smiling and people will wonder what you've been doing.

Charlie as Colt Revolver Jr. in

Taming the Wild, Wild, West

2007

Chapter Ten

My Scrapbook

PASCO
Chamber of Commerce
& THE PORT OF PASCO

Agriculture Hall of Fame

The Agriculture Hall of Fame was formed in 2000 to recognize and honor those individuals that have made significant contributions to the agricultural community in Franklin County. Nominees from neighboring counties outlying Franklin County will also be considered. A selection committee made of representatives from the agricultural community will review all nomination packages.

To date, over 25 individuals have been inducted into the Hall of Fame. Candidates will be judged on their contribution to improving agricultural practices and must stand out among their peers because of their community involvement and unselfish community service activities. All selected individuals and their families will be recognized at the Pasco Ag Show. The Ag Hall of Fame inductions will be presented at a special gala and program following the 2010 Ag Show.

Farmers, growers, ranchers, and owners/employees of agribusiness firms are all eligible for nomination.

Agriculture Hall of Fame Nomination Form

Nominee's Name: **Charles F. (Charlie) Card**
Mailing Address: **7102 S. Steele Rd**
Street Address: **Prosser, WA 99350**
Nominee's Phone: **509-786-4990** house E-Mail:
Date of Birth: **Jan 12, 1937**   Birthplace: **Mason City, WA**
Date of Death (if deceased):
Nominator's Name: **Linda Card + Friends**
Phone: **509-788-1005** Fax: E-Mail:
Friend Contact: **Gail Matsumura**
Phone: **509-788-0994** Fax: E-Mail:

This is still a surprise!

Charlie Card ①

Introduction:
It is with great joy and pride that we submit Charles F. (Charlie) Card as a nominee for the 2010 Ag Hall of Fame.

Charlie, in his own words, "is an old broken down lineman who likes to grow grass and raise cows."

In this phase of his life Charlie has become fully involved with agriculture and livestock and promotes them wherever he may be.

Life Story:
   Family History

   Charlie Card was born Jan 12, 1937 at Mason City, WA to Leland and Helen Card. Helen being a homemaker and Leland (Red) an ~~equipment~~ skinner ~~rider~~ on Grand Coulee Dam, this made Charlie a "dam brat."
   After 4 years at Lone Pine the family moved into Chelan where Red had an auto electric shop. Life was good for red headed Charlie a stones throw from Lake Chelan. He had a reputation around town as being a "busy little boy."
   Life took a turn for the worse when about 1950 the family moved to San Marcos, Calif., at least in the eyes of a 13 year old boy.
   While in Calif. they had an assortment of milk cows, fowl, and small animals. It was a typical small acreage of its day.
   At the very mature age of

16 Charlie and a buddy decided they had enough of Calif and its schools and they lit out for Texas in an <u>ancient</u> car. They limped into Dayton, Texas, where the buddy had family. Finishing the school year was enough of Texas for Charlie. He hitchhiked home — to Chelan.

In those days a kid could always find work and Charlie had no trouble. He worked all summer and started high school in Chelan in the fall. A batchelor boy living in an old shack. He had more escapades than one kid should be allowed. The saying "It takes a village to raise a kid" probably originated with Charlie Card. The town of Chelan kept him busy. Merchants had work for him. When he finished up at <u>Fosters</u> Meat Market he went to Harton's service station until closing up.

2.

The town did their best to keep him busy. Uncle Earl, the town constable, kept a watchful eye on him too.

Much to the townsfolks delight Charlie Card graduated from Chelan High School in 1955.

Uncle Sam had his number and he entered the U.S. Army in June of 1955. He made a good combat engineer, running cat. After numerous building and tearing down bridges across the Rhine, in Germany, he was honorably discharged and returned to Chelan in 2 years.

Never idle for long, he had plenty of jobs but decided to go to school at CWCE (Central Washington College of Education) in Ellensburg. (Now known as Central W. Univ.). Work and the usual major - girls - got in the way and he only did 2 years at Central.

After an assortment of jobs and farming on the side Charlie hired on with Chelan Co. PUD at Rock Island Dam as a temporary. He progressed away from the dam into the line department. Up the ladder from a grunt to a journeyman lineman. He retired as a serviceman from Chelan Co PUD in 1992 with 30 years service. Many of these years were spent farming on the side, either at his brother-in-laws ~~place~~ ranch in the Antoine or on a small peach orchard he had. Raising his family, finance committee of his church, boy scout leader, junior rodeo chairman, and good neighbor are a few of the things that kept Charlie Card busy.

    Charlie left the Wenatchee area and moved to Prosser. There he met a gal, Linda, who had a small acreage, a few cows, and a couple saddle horses.

Things progressed, they got hitched, and the work commenced.

Cow numbers increased, more land was aquired, more and better methods were learned.

It hat one of them didn't think of the other one did and life has been real busy. The are still learning and trying to do better.

Accomplishments:

One of a man's greatest accomplishments in life is to help and encourage others along the path of life. If you can help to educate and produce productive citizens for our nation, and people who will think, you have done well.

To be thought well of by the people you know and your neighbors.

In the livestock industry, to produce a quality product for human consumption using modern methods and being a good steward of the land and animals.

A wise old gentleman who had more cattle in one day than we will have forever gave us this piece of advice. "Find a niche and fill it." I think Charlie Card has done a good job of finding his niche and filling it.

Community Involvement

In his earlier life, in Wenatchee, Charlie helped build his church building. He worked before and after work and long hours on the week end taking charge of the crews. He was instrumental in obtaining heavy equipment for setting trusses etc.

He worked with the boy scouts.

Charlie was an organizer of the Junior Rodeo Association in the Douglas/Chelan County area from about 1980-1987.

Charlie joined the Benton County Cattlemens Assn in 1994. He has been very active locally as well as in the Washington Cattlemen Assoc.

In 2003 Charlie was a spokesman for the livestock industry during the BSE episode in Mabton

Over the years Charlie has made many trips to Olympia on behalf of the livestock industry, and agriculture in general, speaking out for property rights. Legislative Days for the Cattlemen and Beef in the Capitol are attended whenever possible.

Around 2003-07 Dr. Doug Walsh and Dr. Holly Ferguson, WSU-Prosser conducted studies on our place of horn flies and face flies life cycles.

2006 Steve Fransen hosted an irrigated pasture training seminar at our place.

2007 USDA hosted a delegation from the Republic of Georgia. They asked if these folks could come to our place. It was a memorable experience for all.

Charlie has been asked by several educators to speak to their continuing education classes on pasture management. They usually run overtime.

2008 We completed a WSU Tilling the Soil of Opportunity Class.

Summer of 2008 Charlie played Colt Revolver Jr. in the Valley Theater Co's presentation of Taming the Wild Wild West — in a Dress. This melodrama had record attendance and many people came just to see Charlie Card.

Many grazing seminars and field days have been attended. The prelude to WA Cattlemens Convention, Cattlemens College is some of the best education you can get.

Our neighborhood has block watch. Charlie Card is known as the watchdog. He keeps an eye on the whole neighborhood. If somebody is "out of place" he is checking as to what they are doing there. One particular vehicle spent to long where he didn't belong. Charlie approached him as to why. After much hemming and hawing he fessed up that he was a police officer and was watching a place.

Recognition

Charlie Cord hasn't recieved much formal recognition. He just does it.

He wears a belt buckle he recieved from the Jr. Rodeo Assn. when he retired as chairman in 1987.

He and Linda both have WCA belt buckles for selling the most memberships in the WCA for the years 1997, 1998, and 2002 and 2003.

Organization Listings

Since about 1994 Charlie has been active in Benton Co. Cattlemens. He has been on various committees.
- Vice Pres 1997-98
- Elected pres of BCCA 1999-2001
- Has been both a County and state Cattlemens director.
- 2002-2006 WA Cattlemens Assoc Dist 5 Representative Benton, Franklin, Klickitat and Yakima Counties.
- Farm Forum and Ag Show participant since 1997
- Has worked with Farm Fair since about 1999

Were You There Charlie?

Ag Hall of Fame Sponsor

Ronald J. Perkins, CPA
Baker & Giles, CPAS
Tippett Company of Washington
Gary and Lori Middleton
South Columbia Basin Irrigation District
Louis Meissner

Cake Sponsor

Tonie Neff and Sandy Johnson

A Special Thanks to

The Greater Pasco Area
Chamber of Commerce Staff
Nikki Gerds, Executive Director
Steve Lee, Office Manager
Columbia Basin College
Sight and Sound Services
Bob Kreider, Owner
Richard Burger
The Country Gentlemen Restaurant & Catering Staff
Laura Smith and Linda Nitzman
Wonderful Weddings Decorations
Inna Juarez, Owner
Lucky Flowers
Ben & Melissa Barlow / Tiffany Wright
Owners
Viokes Fresh Market Bakery "Pasco"
Herrington Trophies
Preston Premium Wines
Jesse Fleicher "Guitar Soloist"

2010 Nominees

Mid Columbia Ag Hall of Fame – Pioneer
Bill and Norma Bennett
William Cabler
Jim O'Connor
Shannon McDaniel
Florence Thompson
Charlie Card
Warren and Audrey Clifford

Agriculture Advisory Leadership Award
Lyle Hult
Rich Cummins
Bob Olexa

Agribusiness Man/Woman of the Year
James Bacon
Cheryn Preston

The Greater Pasco Area Chamber of Commerce and the Port of Pasco are proud to honor our farmers who have helped create a rich heritage of agriculture in the Columbia Basin. They have made this area what it is today—a growing, thriving, diverse and vibrant community.

The Port of Pasco and
The Greater Pasco Area
Chamber of Commerce
Presents

**10th Annual
Agriculture
Hall of Fame
Gala**

Thursday, January 7th, 2010

2010 Mid Columbia Ag Hall of Fame

Individuals that have been actively involved in the Agriculture industry in our area over a period of many years, donated their time to community activities (unselfish acts), served on a variety of boards and commissions or assisted often.

Honoree Inductees:

Bud Mercer

Ron and Rella Reiman / Porky (Ralph) Thomsen
"T&R Farms"

2010 Ag Advisory Leadership Award

An award given to an individual active in the Agriculture Industry that has a great influence in the Agriculture industry and community through their leadership presence and community involvement.

Inductee:

Tim and Marlene Tippett

2010 Agribusiness Man/Women of the Year

Given each annual admirable community involvement, technology advancement, trade/s who have noticeably enhanced the agricultural industry – local and global.

Inductee:

Steve Cooper

2010 Ag Hall of Fame Committee
Gary Middleton
Ed Alex
Louie Messmer
Henry Johnson
Missy N. Hill
Bob Tippett
Nick Cox
Monica Van Hollebeke
Terry Fleschmann

6:00pm – 7:00pm   Social Hour

Entertainment   Jesse Fletcher "Guitar Soloist"

7:00pm

Master of Ceremonies   Opening Comments
                        Jim Twomey, Executive Director, Port of Pasco

Invocation   Walter Neff, Owner/Operator Neff Ranches

DINNER

Recognition of Sponsors and Special Guests ... Jim Twomey
Recognition of Standing Scholarships .... Gary Middleton
Recognition of Past Inductees .... Gary Middleton

2nd Annual Les Schwab Ag Hall of Fame Scholarship Award

SCHOLARSHIP PRESENTATION
"Columbia Basin College"

Presenter   Les Schwab

PRESENTATION OF PLAQUES

Presenter
Honoree   Bud Mercer
Presenter
Honoree   Ron & Rella Reiman / Porky (Ralph) Thomsen
                         "T&R Farms"

Presenter   Henry Johnson

Ag Advisor
Presenter   Tim and Marlene Tippett
                                                  Bob Tippett

Agribusiness Man/Women
Presenter   Steve Cooper
                                              Gary Middleton

Presenter
                         MYSTERY AWARD
                                              To Be Announced

---

Agriculture Hall of Fame Past Inductees

1st Annual – November 18th, 2000
Captain Gray
Walter LaFarge
Reggie Neff
Russell Smith
Daniel Popoff
Gus Jelly
B.B. Horrigan
Cyril Hays

2nd Annual – November 17th, 2001
Charles E. Allard
Chrysler Allard
Don & Alice Dodd
O.C.W. (Chey) Neff
Mary Raimondi

3rd Annual – November 16th, 2002
Lyle
Bill Preston
James Rogers

4th Annual – November 15th, 2003
Mel Morrison
Glenn Whitley

5th Annual – January 8th, 2004
Jack & Donna Williams
Clearance & Helen Cox
Don & Jerome Bauermeister

6th Annual – January 29th, 2005
Louie Messmer
Erwin Easterday
Bill C. Tan

7th Annual – January 29th, 2007
Frank C. Tan
Robert W. Middleton
Paul & Sally Oberbilling

8th Annual – January 19th, 2008
Richard R. (Dick) Moore
Herman F. Achziehr
Walter Burgens

9th Annual – January 17th, 2009
James Vander Flerting
Steve Paisley
Edwin & June Danz
Leonard & Marilyn Andrews

HALL OF FAME (Pioneer Award)
Charlie Card

An ambassador for agriculture. A patient teacher. A selfless volunteer. A cattleman.

Those are all apt descriptions for Prosser resident Charlie Card, and just some of the reasons why he is just the kind of man deserving of induction into the Mid-Columbia Ag Hall of Fame. By nature, Charlie is a promoter of agriculture and the cattle industry he so loves. It's part of his personality – the man can't help himself. He even has patience for the sometimes challenging role as a spokesperson for the industry for local media, always willing to do an interview whether times are good or bad for the cattle industry.

Charlie is a faithful volunteer, showing up to events of all kind, from serving beef at the Cougar Gridiron Classic football game each year, to sharing his wisdom with 5th-graders at the annual Farm Fair event, to years of service on the local and state Cattleman's associations.

He's a man quick to help a neighbor in need and a mentor seeking out students to help on the farm, teaching them his tireless work ethic along the way. He's admired for his interest in agriculture research and his ability to explain modern ranching to audiences of all kinds and his understanding of the process when it is lobbying time in Olympia. And, of course, he raises great cattle.

Charlie was once in line at the grocery store where the man in line in front of him was buying chicken. Charlie quickly informed the man that chicken was for "sissies" and he should be eating beef, instead. That man became Charlie's friend, learning how to raise cattle. And when illness sent the man to the hospital, Charlie was there for the family to make sure the steers got to market and the family got a check.

The broad appreciation for Charlie is easily seen in the letters supporting his nomination to the Hall of Fame. They were written by state senators, cattle industry leaders, FFA advisors, a reporter, friends and a young man Charlie put to work on the ranch as a teen-ager and then helped send to college. The vast support is a testament to a life lived the right way and the impact that one man in a cowboy hat can have on a community.

WCA Ketch Pen - Jan 2011

Save The Date

2011 MID-COLUMBIA AG HALL OF FAME
Thursday, January 20, 2011
Pasco Red Lion Medallion Ballroom
2525 N 20th Ave Pasco, WA
6:00pm Social Hour 7:00pm Dinner
$50.00 Individual or $360 Table of Eight
RSVP (509) 547-9755 RSVP@PASCOCHAMBER.ORG
Be a Part of History!

Charlie Card will be recieving the "The Pioneer Award" at the Mid-Columbia Ag Hall of Fame. The award is given to "those who have significantly influenced agriculture with groundbreaking ideas, participation and leadership, and have displayed advocacy or unselfish acts in their communities" and Charlie has exceeded all of the above qualifications.

CONGRATULATIONS CHARLIE!

Lower Valley cattle rancher headed for Mid-Columbia Ag Hall of Fame

Linda & Charlie
January 2010 when Charlie inducted into the Agriculture Hall of Fame

Charlie & Linda - Spring 2003

Were You There Charlie?

Linda & Charlie, 1999
First Christmas in new home in Prosser

Prosser 1997

Charlie and Whitey 2006

Charlie and Whitey and Jock 20

CARD FAMILY

Chase and Card could be Irish and Dutch

Edwin O. Card **Married** **Ruth Chase**

Born in Tracy Creek, New York

Trade: Engineer

Buried: Fraternal Cemetery - Chelan, WA

Gravestone says: J.E. Card - 1842 - 1917

Born In Lodi, Wisconsin

She died about 1915

Buried in Wisconsin?

They Had One Child - Jonathan Edward Card

Edwin and Jonathan went to Chicago World's Fair in the late 1880's.

Great Grandmother

Ruth Chase

CRAIG FAMILY

Craig is Scotch

Azro Craig

Maternal Great Grandfather of Charlie

Profession: Cook

Buried in Wisconsin

Elizabeth Fick

Maternal Great Grandmother of Charlie

Born in Illinois

Buried in Wisconsin

Children:

Abigail Craig Gregg

Ida Craig Rogers

Henry Craig (Homesteader, Antoine WA)

Ella Iva Craig Card

Emerson Craig (WWI)

Sylvia Craig Behm

Jonathan Edward Card Married Ella Iva Craig

Paternal Grandfather of Charlie   09/09/1901   Paternal Grandmother of Charlie

in Chippewa Falls

Born In Chippewa Falls, Wisconsin

Birth: 02/02/1877

Profession: Trained Accountant

Worked in Seattle on Lake Washington ship canal.

Retired from Chelan Transfer (Truck Driver/Mechanic)

Born in Chippewa Falls, Wisconsin

Birth: 02/16/1879

Profession: Homemaker

Death: October 13, 1941 (Heart Attack while on hunting trip with son-in-law, Roma Spray.)

Death: 1953 (Cancer)

Children:

Ezra Edward	07/1902 to 11/02/1902	Seattle, WA
Elizabeth Ruth	08/05/1904 to 03/14/1984	Chelan, WA.
Bernice Marie	02/10/1906 - 1999	Seattle, WA.
Loren William	11/3/1908 - 1984	Ranch in Antoine, Okanogan. WA.
Leland Henry	**11/3/1908 - 10/13/1996**	**Ranch in Antoine, Okanogan , WA.**
Caroline Hiley	12/11/1909 - 1953	Ranch in Antoine, Okanogan, WA.
Lyda Verona	11/02/1912 - 2016	Ranch in Antoine, Okanogan, WA.
Chester Emerson	02/29/1916 - 1987	Chelan, WA.
Ella Mae	09/08/1922 - 12/1922	Chelan, WA.

And Their Children's Children

Elizabeth Ruth Card   Married 02/28/1923   Roma Albert Spray

Children:

Roma Albert Jr. 07/02/1925 - 07/13/1925

Wayne Edward   Married 06/11/1944   Glenna Faye DeWalt

04/30/1924 – 12/09/2011   09/21/1925 – 08/30/2020

Children:

Donna Marie 11/10/1945 Married 01/05/2008 Bruce Schmutzler 12/07/1944

Children:

Kathy Kemp 05/07/1973 Married Allan Kemp 05/24/2003

Janis Louise 07/05/1948

Children:

Lisa 01/19/1973

Angela 09/14/1976

Douglas Wayne 10/08/1951 Married Jacquie 03/29/1952

Children:

Brittany 04/28/1989

Rodney Glen 12/25/1954 Married Kim 12/27/1956

Children:

Jeremiah 04/29/1987

Michael 11/07/1983

Eunice Marie Lewis 11/28/1926 – 08/15/2021 Married 08/26/1966 Harvey Lewis

(2nd husband)

Children:

Judith Darlene 8/30/1946

Michael Roma 8/1/1947

Patsy Lou 12/25/1949

Vicki Lynn 11/1/1951 Married Lester Ramsvig

Steven Lewis 01/12/1953

Ronald Harvey 01//22/1933 - 11/11/1971

Genevieve Ruth 07/03/1934 Married 02/01/1964 Laurence Carl Knorr

Children:

Leih Ann 11/25/1969 - Deceased

Bernice Marie Hughs Married 04/28/1920 Darwin Godfry Hughes (died in 1980)

Children:

Carlysle   Married   Hope

    Children:

    Kathie (1957) Married Johnny Green

        Children:

        Elizabeth (1984)

        Michelle (1987)

Gerald (Jerry) Married Rowena Leep

    Children:

    Anne (Schappert)

    John

        Children:

        Elizabeth

        David

Janet Marie   Married George Foy

    Children:

    Sherry Noyes'

        Children:

        Greg

        Sandra

Loren William Card   Married   Lena

    Children:

Nikki (1940)   Adopted in Alaska

Charlie Card

Hannah Ruth   02/03/19 Married Remington Bedgood

09/04/15

Children:

Dameon 02/19
Bonnie Marie 11/21/1998

Caroline Joy   11/15/2000

Emily Grace   09/20/2002 - 10/31/09

David Thomas 12/13/20

John Leland 06/29/1967   Married 06/06/2004 Rachel Coen

Dominican Republic

Children:

Rebecca Grace 04/26/2005

John & Steven 05/30/2006 - 05/30/2006

Emma Grace 08/07/2007

Linda Marie 11/10/1944   Married 12/21/68   Stephen Thomason

Children:

Joel Patrick 09/24/1970 Married 06/01/1995 Cristina

Children:

Serra Kaylin   11//11/1997

Julia Suzanna 01/06/2001

Jarred Steven 10/31/2003

Steven James 11/17/2006

Daniel Wayne 11/11/1972 Married 08/03/2002 Nikki divorced

Children:

Samuel 05/23/2003

Gabriel 08/2005 Married Janet

Jacob 08/19/1979   Married 09/24/2005   Kelly Segerstrom

no children

GloryEllen 08/29/1981

Hiley (Caroline) Married   Earl Bryant

   Children:

Roger Earl   10/1934

Paul   Drowned in a hot tub due to an epileptic seizure

Verona (Lyda)   Married 04/20/1938   David Franklin

Chelan, WA

   Children:

Richard 1944   Married   Sharon

Children:

Darek

Amy

Chester (Chet) Edward   Married   Clarene Crawford

Master Seargent

US Army

No Children

NOTE REGARDING GENEOLOGY:

Done from family hearsay and not verified to public records.

Leland Henry Card	**Married**	**Mary Helen Petersen**
11/3/1908 - 10/13/1996	10/8/1935	04/28/1910 – 02/14/07
Charlie's Father	At parent's home on Wapato St. next door to Christian Church Chelan, WA.	Charlie's Mother

Children:

Charles Fredrick 01/12/1937   Married 1958   Cassie Zornes

Married 1996   Linda

Children (Adopted):

Patrician Ann 06/30/1966

Michael 07/31/1968   Married 9/11/93   Jennifer

Children:

Eric   06/08/1998

Matthew 11/22/1999

Bonnie Jean 05/23/1942   Married 11/17/62   Thomas Edmund Cobb

Escondido, CA   03/10/1939 - 07/03 2011

Children:

Sandra Jean - 09/02/1964   Married 8/19/1989   Stephen Glenn Midgley

Los Angeles, CA

Children:

William Jedadiah 05/19/1993

Samuel John   03/21/1995

Grandma Petersen at X-Bar-J Ranch – Elbow Lake - 08/1954

Were You There Charlie?

A note from Linda on Charlie's cancer journey

In May of 2016 Charlie was diagnosed with Cecal Cancer (Colon). On June 3, 2016 he underwent a right robotic hemicolectomy. In regular language that means they took out a piece of his colon on the right side and reconnected it to the small intestine. He recovered well with a confirmed diagnosis of cancer and 11 of 15 lymph nodes positive for tumor. The good part was it hadn't spread to other organs.

On July 1 he had his first chemo. First time isn't too bad. On July 5 he had surgery to install a port. That's where they insert the needles when they give you chemotherapy. Quite a way to celebrate our 20th wedding anniversary.

July 8 the second chemo but not in the port – it needs to settle in first. A week off to go fishing in Canada with Cousin Les. Everybody survived and they came home with salmon.

Chemo continued weekly until August. Then Charlie got sick and spent a week in the hospital. Chemo resumed September 2nd. This routine continued until December 20th. Trying to get 6 weeks or so with chemo treatments once a week and keep him out of the hospital monitoring his blood, with CT's and MRI's every so often.

Chemo was over December 20, 2016. After a couple weeks he started feeling like a human being again. This lasted through the first part of February as the scans showed there was no shrinkage in the tumors. The Doctor said he must go back on chemo.

Charlie went back on chemo February 3rd, 2017 for weekly treatments. It was a wild ride. There was a trip to the hospital, a couple of weeks off for medical reasons, endovascular surgery on his leg for blood clots. We thought he was going to lose his foot, but he recovered. Removal of the first joint on his right middle finger due to a hangnail, bleeding mouth, and looking like he had been beaten. During this time there was very little tumor shrinkage and the Doctor kept saying "more, more". All the while feeling awful and not enough energy to hardly carry himself. I was driving him everywhere with 2 trips to Tri-Cities weekly and farming. Life was hell.

Finally, August 28, 2017 Charlie had enough. He told the Doctor he was done with chemo. The Doctor agreed to four months off. All of us thought he would be dead by Christmas and we think he did too.

After a couple of weeks with no poison he started feeling and looking more human. We started considering the alternatives that friends and family had told us about. The first was Essiac Tea, an old Ojibway Indian cure his daughter had told us about. What have you got to lose?

He tries it. Not bad. Dandelion Root Tea - tastes terrible but have heard good about it. Drinks it. Bee Pollen – he was on that awhile but it upset his stomach. Not too long on it. Tri Mushroom Complex he was told about - used that for several months. Cream of Tartar – 1/4 teaspoon in water or juice 2 times a day. This balances the PH in your system. Charlie was on all of this at once for a while.

Back to the story. When he returned to the Doctor for a checkup on December 17, much to the Doctor's surprise the blood test and scans were better with tumor reduction. He has been back every few months since and continues with good tests. Now he is only on Essiac Tea and sometimes Cream of Tartar.

The takeaway? Never give up. Don't feel sorry for yourself. Be positive!

As awful as chemo was, Charlie tried to make the best of it. He visited other patients to tell them a joke or reassure them. He always gave the nurses a bad time. He had his buddies Joe Zamora and Jerry Castilleja. Together they were the "Three Amigos". Both Joe and Jerry were younger than Charlie and both lost their battle but they each encouraged the others.

We have eternal gratitude to Cesar and family for seeing us through this trial. No matter what, they were there for us. The little kids really came into their own. Feeding cattle in the winter when nobody was home and doing what needed done.

It is now October 2021. Charlie is still here. Older. Slower. But just as ornery.

- Linda Card

A Prayer for Later Years

Author Unknown

Lord, thou knowest that I am growing older.

Keep me from becoming too talkative, and particularly keep me from falling into the tiresome habit of expressing an opinion on every subject.

Release me from the craving to straighten out everybody's affairs. Keep my mind free from the recital of endless details. Give me wings to get to the point.

Give me grace, dear Lord, to listen to others describe their aches and pains. Help me endure the boredom with patience and keep my lips sealed, for my own aches and pains are increasing in number and intensity, and the pleasure of discussing them is becoming sweeter as the years go by.

Teach me the glorious lesson that, occasionally, I might be mistaken. Keep me reasonably sweet. I do not wish to be a saint (saints are so hard to live with), but a sour old person is the work of the devil.

Make me thoughtful, but not moody; helpful, but not pushy;

independent, yet able to accept with graciousness favors that others wish to bestow on me.

Free me of the notion that simply because I have lived a long time, I am wiser than those who have not lived so long.

If I do not approve of some of the changes that have taken place in recent years, give me the wisdom to keep my mouth shut.

Lord knows that when the end comes, I would like to have a friend or two left.

The Ultimate Workbook
for Preserving Your Legacy & You

Write Heart Memories®

Beth Lord

Available on www.bethlord.com & www.amazon.com Online Support Step by Step

The Easy Way To Get Your Stories In A Book.

Write Heart Memories®

Beth

Beth Lord
Story Guide, Author, Therapist, and Founder
Write Heart Memories® Publishing Company

206.929.0024 | www.bethlord.com

beth@bethlord.com

Made in the USA
Columbia, SC
07 April 2022